AF593857

The Jungle Paintings

Henri Rousseau

The Jungle Paintings
Henri Rousseau

With an introduction
by Harald Eggebrecht

Tate Publishing

This edition first published 2005 by order of the Tate Trustees
by Tate Publishing a division of Tate Enterprises Ltd,
Millbank, London SW1P 4RG
www.tate.org.uk/publishing

British Library Cataloguing in Publication Data
A catalogue record for this book is available from the British Library

A Schirmer/Mosel Production
Lithography: Scan Color, Leipzig
Design: Klaus E. Göltz, Halle
Printing and binding: Gorenjski Tisk, Kranj
Translation: Anthea Bell

ISBN 1-85437-640-3

Jungle Fever

HARALD EGGEBRECHT

Everyone knows that Mexico
is an imaginary country.
GÜNTER EICH

'Jungle' is one of the most magical of words. It sounds like an incantation rising from the dark, hot depths of the tropics, where crocodiles lurk in the water and beautiful orchids flower in the ancient trees, while giant butterflies spread their shimmering wings and flutter, reeling, amidst heavy scents and perfumes. It is a seductive word too: speaking of strange desires and delights it lures you deeper into the forest, to the Africa-tinged world of Tarzan the ape-man, to Mowgli the wolf-boy in his Indian setting, and King Kong the giant gorilla who inhabits a similar wilderness on a distant, fantastic island. 'Jungle' is also a word of fear, of horror, of nightmare, a word signifying death and destruction, poison and downfall, eating and being eaten.

*

Such are the associations conjured up when we enter the big glasshouses of a botanical garden and breathe the hot, humid air. The atmosphere is instantly full of scents so heavy and intense they seem tangible. Only then does the eye, surprised and apprehensive, move to plants that many of us keep in miniature form on the windowsill at home, but that now tower above us, giants of the vegetable kingdom. When assembled at home, such a collection of plants, with its cacti, orchids, camellias and hibiscus, its rubber plants, grasses and ferns, represents the beginnings of a mini-jungle; we are trying to lay out our own botanical garden. If little figures and souvenirs are arranged among these pot plants we have created an exotic little Rousseau-esque tableau.

*

Henri Rousseau, who described himself as one of France's 'best realist painters' was considered naive or even primitive by conservative art critics because of his poor command of academic technique, from the handling of proportion to the sacrosanct principle of central perspective. But despite his personally gentle disposition, his modesty and kindness, and his inclination towards bourgeois and even reactionary ideas of order, Rousseau was extremely self-confident, and firmly convinced of the high value of his art. He had a direct and immediate affinity with exotic plants, which his imagination turned to towering walls and ramparts of vegetation, symphonies in green, with dramatic touches provided by great cats bringing down buffalo, attacking human beings, or simply lying in wait for prey. Even the monkeys that appear in many of his pictures never seem just amusing or cute; there is always something wild and anarchic about them.

Rousseau did not deny the apocryphal tale that he had served in the army in Mexico when Napoleon III made the Archduke Maximilian of Austria emperor of that country (a venture into power politics on the part of the French ruler that ended disastrously with Maximilian's execution by firing squad). The artist thus never expressly contradicted the myth that he had seen exotic landscapes for himself, had breathed the air of Central America, and had some knowledge of such foreign climes. In his jungle pictures, Rousseau's alleged experience of Mexico proved in fact to be influenced by his visits to the Botanical Gardens and World Expositions in Paris, where exotic plant species were on display. He constructed his dangerously beautiful tropical forests as compact specimens of pictorial architecture designed to suit the building plans of his imagination. The landscapes he depicted were not real, but remained faithful to his own ideas of the jungle, seen by the characteristic livid light of his blood-red suns and bright yellow moons, which cast almost no shadows.

Rousseau thus became the creator of his own jungle, and he almost encyclopaedically arranged, intensified and intermingled the many shades of green in its leaves and trees, ferns and gigantic creepers. There can be no geographical constraints on such imaginative activity. It seems quite natural to see an American Indian fighting a gorilla here, a Siberian tiger bringing down an African buffalo, a Parisian lady going for a walk in the jungle. It is not surprising that the Surrealists valued Rousseau's freedom of thought and invention.

Yet Rousseau was not just a dreamer, and he did not aim for alienation in a Symbolist sense; instead, he wanted to construct his dream pictures realistically, giving them monumentally concrete form as he fixed them firmly on canvas. Not even the far from innocent, dark and eerie riddles posed by such pictures as *The Sleeping Gypsy* 1897,

The Snake Charmer 1907 and *The Dream* 1910 achieve their effect by employing Mannerist artificiality or a wealth of literary allusions. With the same meticulous attention that he paid to constructing his walls of vegetation, where a naked woman lying on a sofa among them looks as 'natural' as an animal, he painted the desert as a background for the sensuality of the sleeping gypsy woman, adding an inquisitive nocturnal visitor in the shape of the lion with its glowing yellow eyes. Ultimately there was no distinction between dream and reality for Rousseau. To him, as a realistic painter *sui generis*, they were one and the same.

*

Lions and tigers, monkeys and luxuriant, exotic vegetation had been depicted in painting long before 'Le Douanier' Rousseau came to portray them. As early as Rubens, orgiastic scenes of hippopotamus and lion hunts aroused similar feelings of mingled fear and delight in the observer. Delacroix too made a careful study of the great cats, and his canvases presented magnificent lion hunts full of symbolism and blazing colour. Exoticism as an artistic mode and fashion flourished in a number of different ways in the eighteenth century, and in the character of the Noble Savage – promoted long before the French Revolution by thinkers including the painter's namesake Jean-Jacques Rousseau, as a natural counterbalance to the perceived sorry state of civilization – it embarked upon a long career, leading to Tarzan, and to the science fiction and fantasy movies of the present day.

*

Yet Rousseau's jungle fever, which is not so feverish after all, excites the observer for the very reason that it conjures up a jungle that resides only in the power of the imagination. It is naive only in so far as it looks back to the primeval fears and temptations of childhood, and expresses them in Rousseau's specifically realistic manner. We all know these terrors: fear of the depths of the forest, whether beech and spruce grow there or palms and gum trees; fear of the bloodcurdling violence that could emerge from those depths in every dreadful form; fear of all that is strange and threatening. Conversely, there is a distinctly erotic urge to press on and explore this mysterious jungle, perhaps coming upon a gingerbread house in the middle of the forest, or the pyramids of the sun god, meeting wicked witches or beguiling fairies – the former wanting to fatten us up and eat us, the latter to offer us three wishes. We feel a yearning for the beauty of what we have never seen, and amazement at the magical power of the Other; we long to wander through the impenetrable wilderness and disappear in it, never to be seen again. And finally, we entertain the seductive notion that beyond the jungle, far from all the constraints of civilisation, there lies a freer, footloose, adventurous life, bound to no programmes, but always surprising and full of variety.

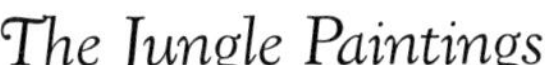

Tiger in a Tropical Storm (Surprised!) 1891
Oil on canvas 130 x 162 CM

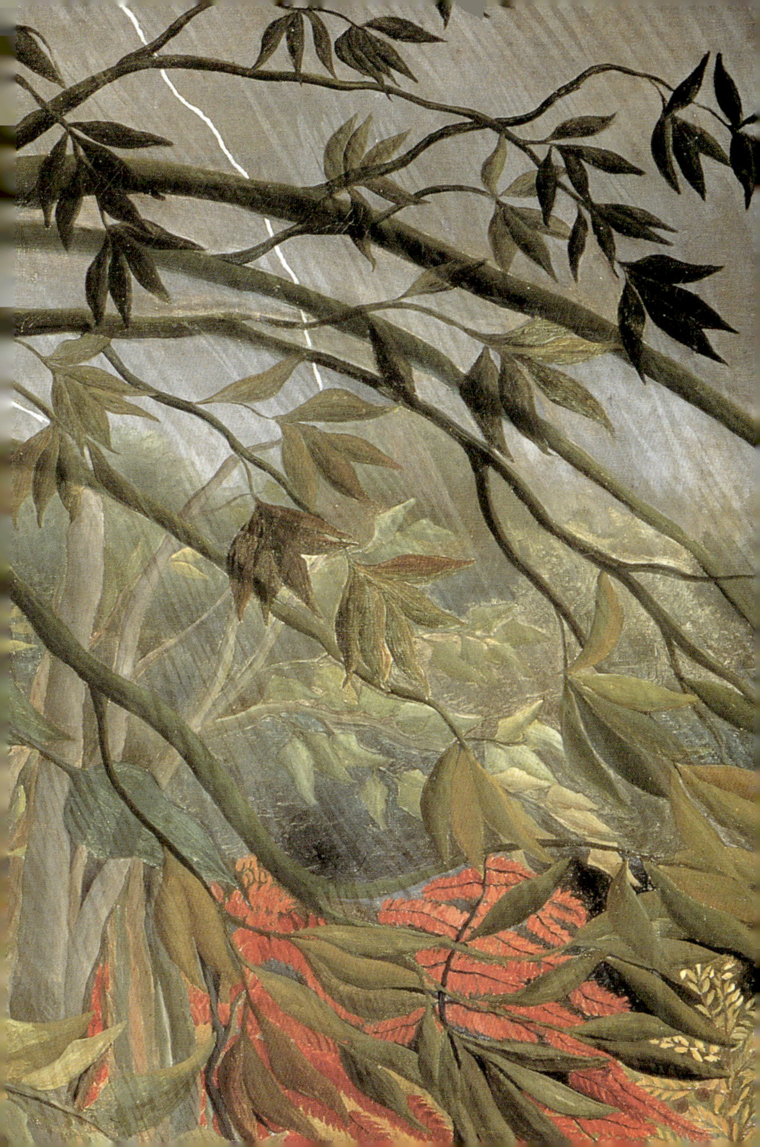

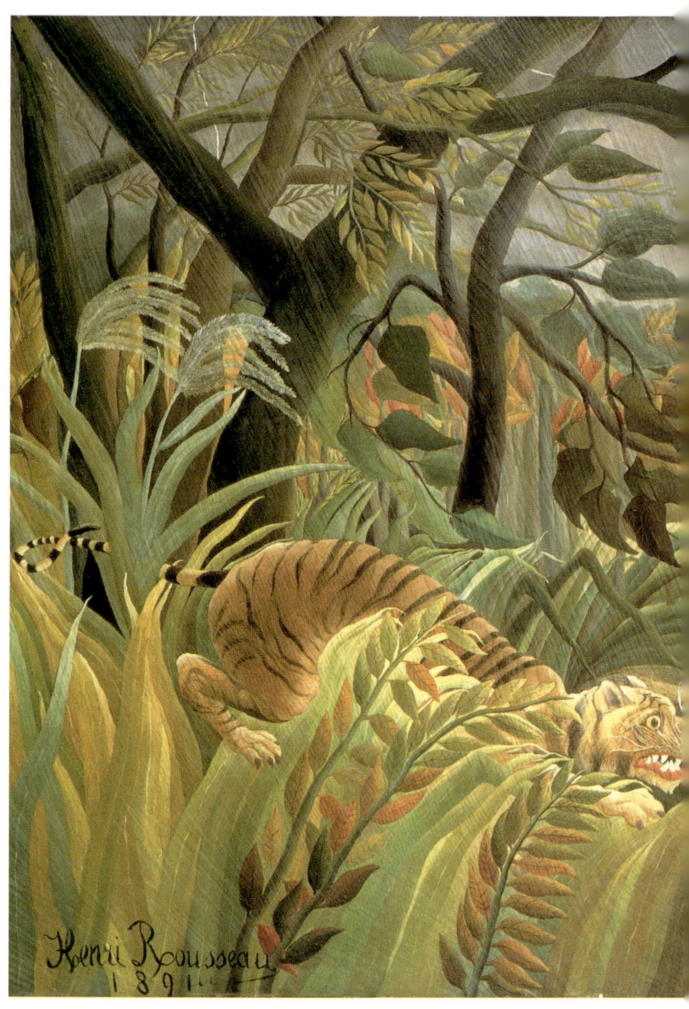
Henri Rousseau
1891

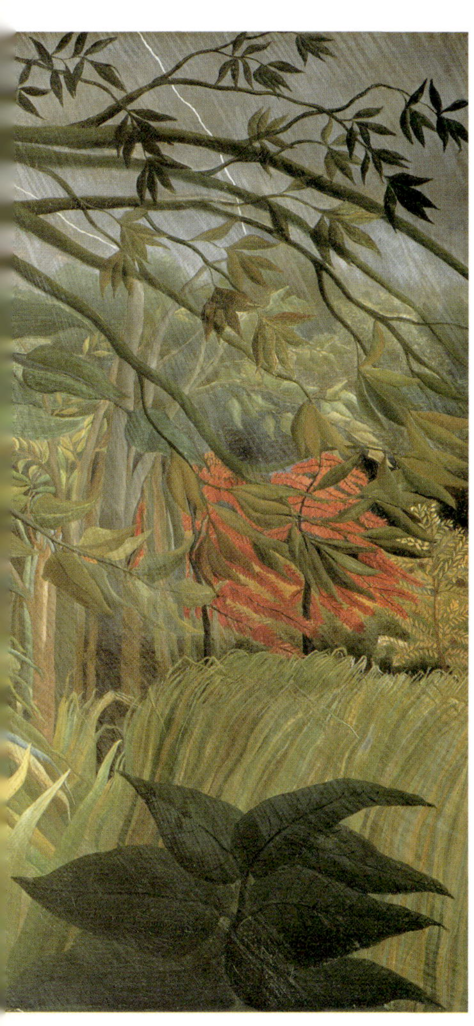

Tiger in a Tropical Storm (Surprised!)
1891

The Hungry Lion Throws Itself on the Antelope 1905
Oil on canvas 200 x 300 cm
(OVERLEAF; DETAIL OPPOSITE)

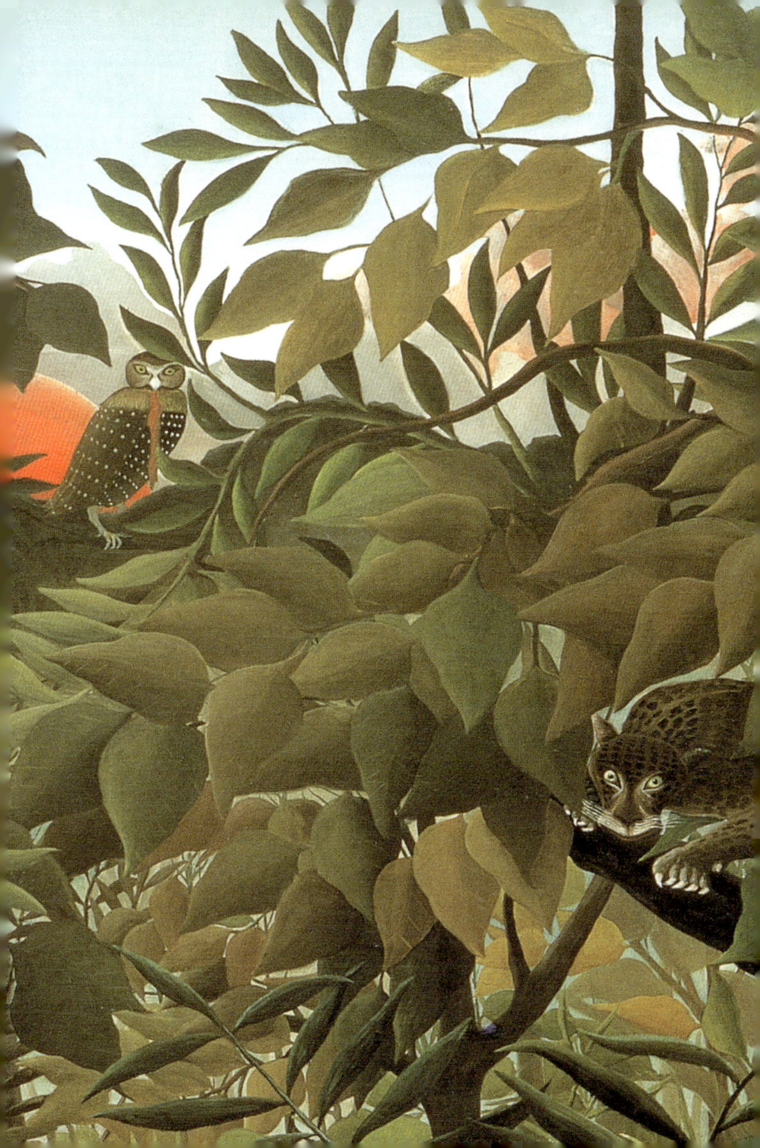

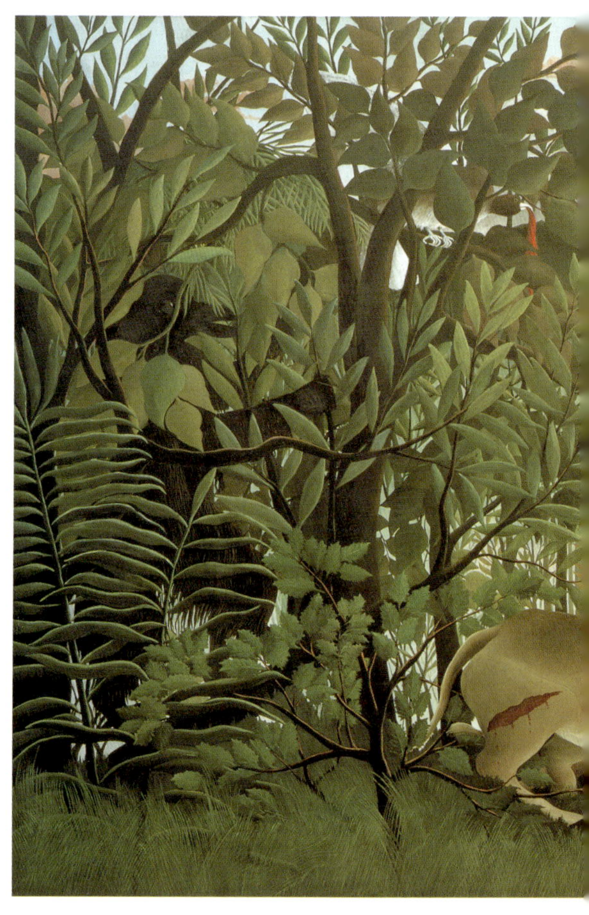

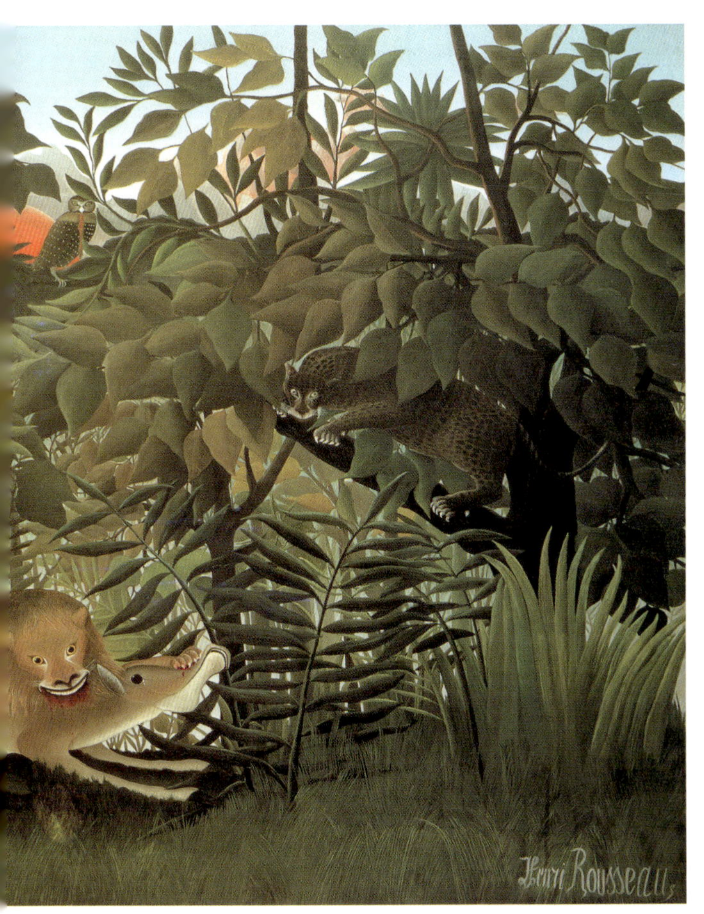
Henri Rousseau

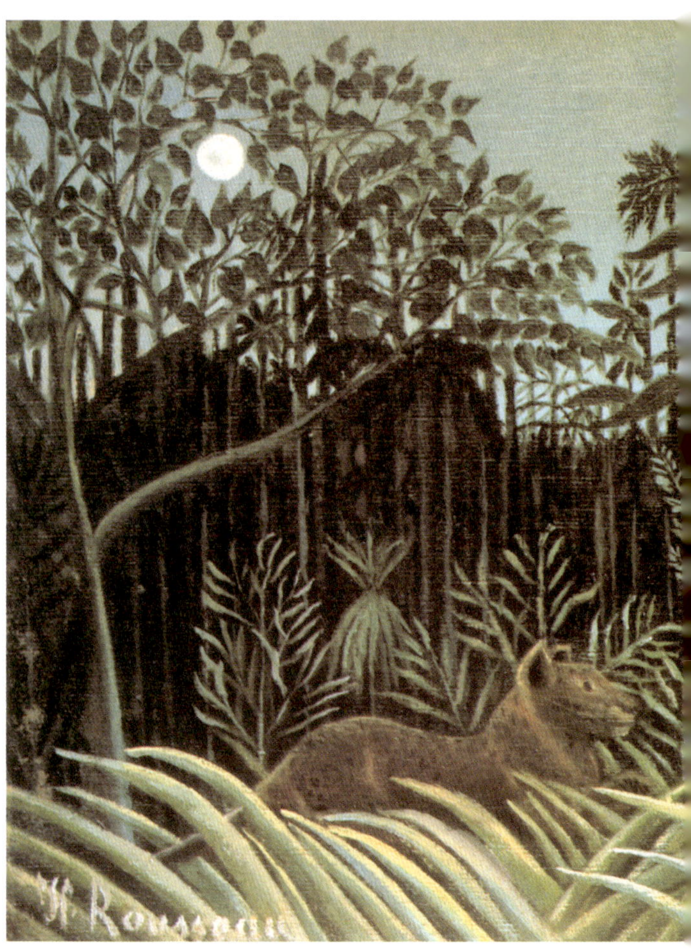
H. Rousseau

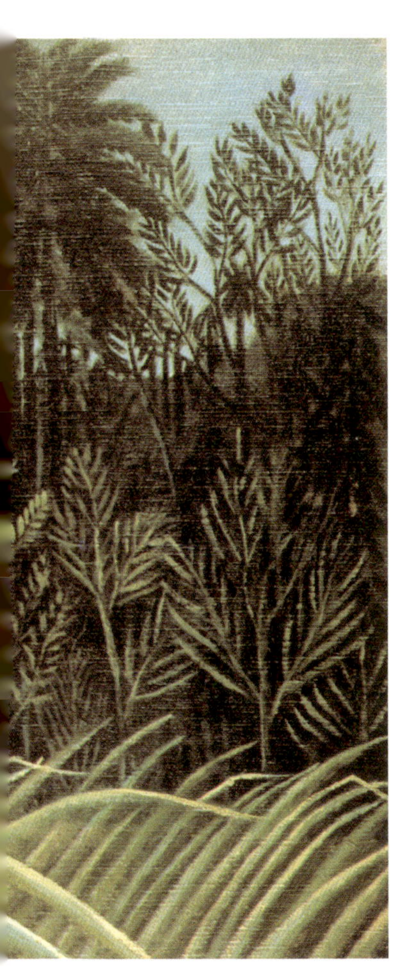

Lion in the Jungle c.1904
Oil on canvas 38.4 x 46.5 CM

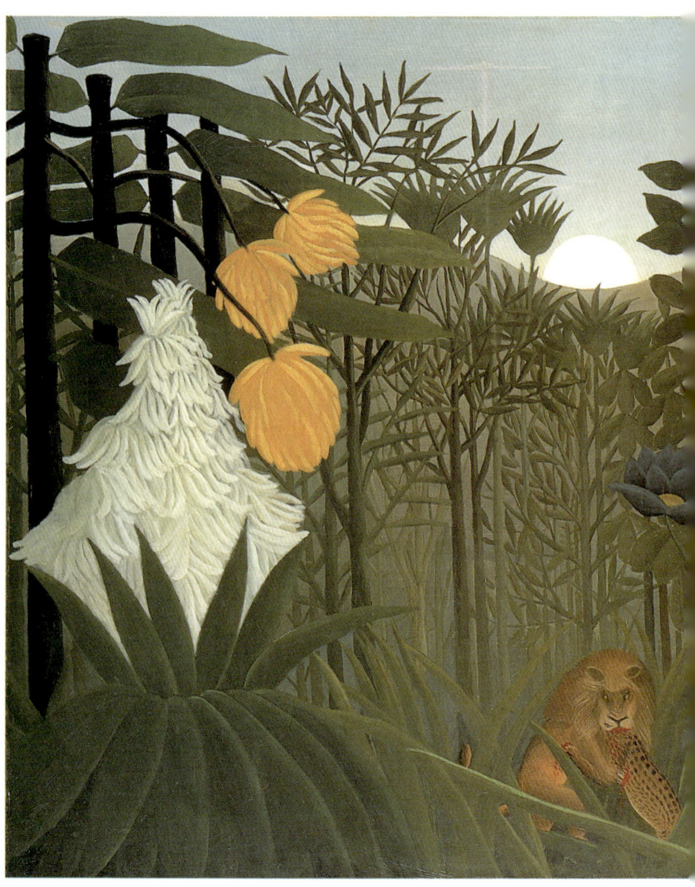

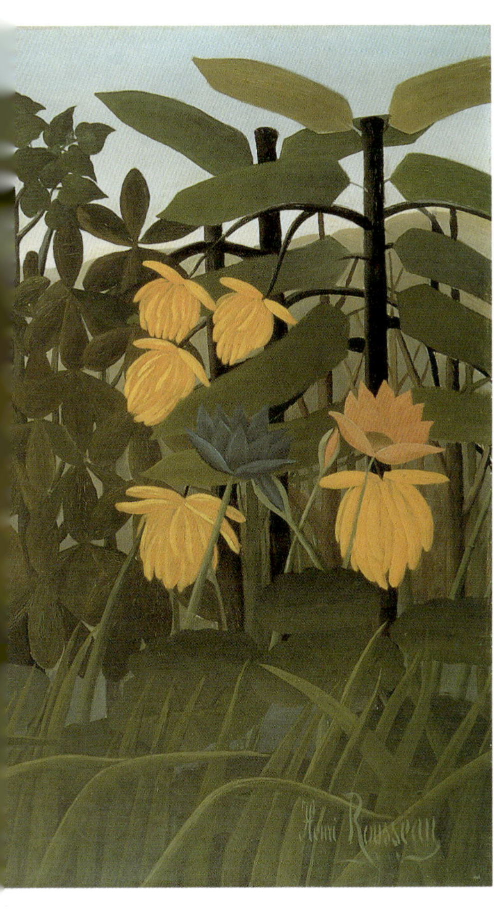

The Lion's Repast
1907
Oil on canvas
113.5 x 160 cm

Fight Between a Tiger and a Buffalo
1908
Oil on fabric 170 x 189.5 CM (DETAIL)

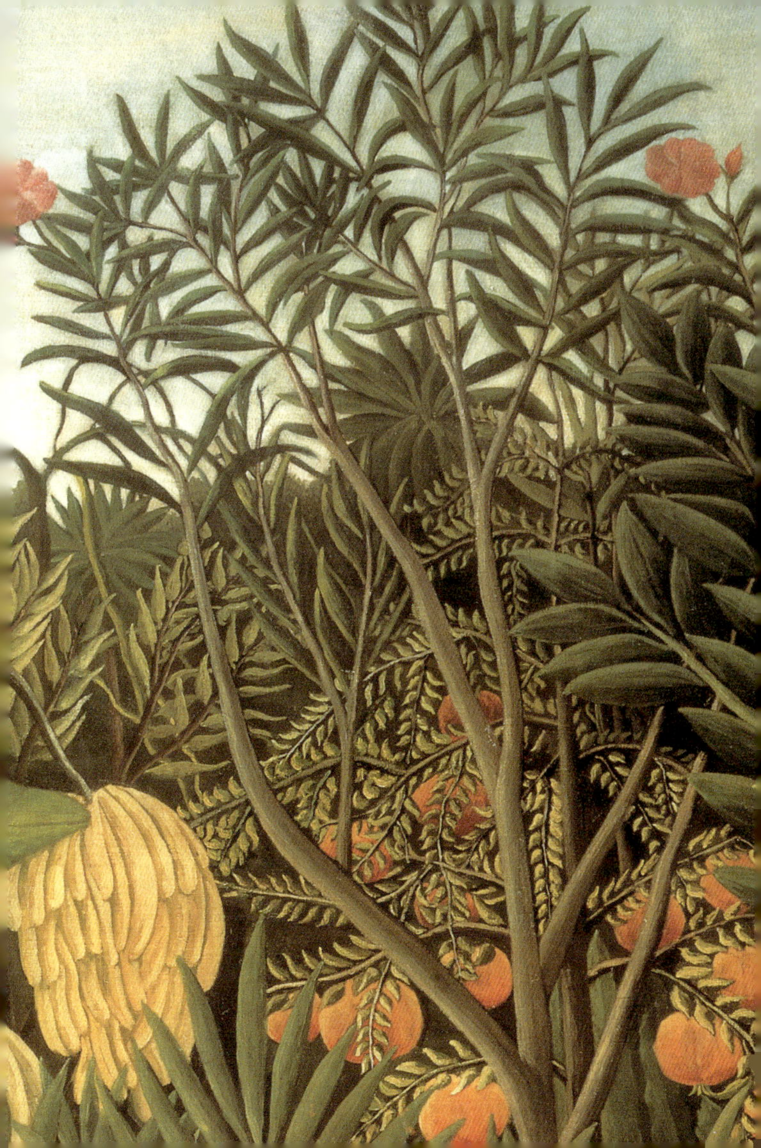

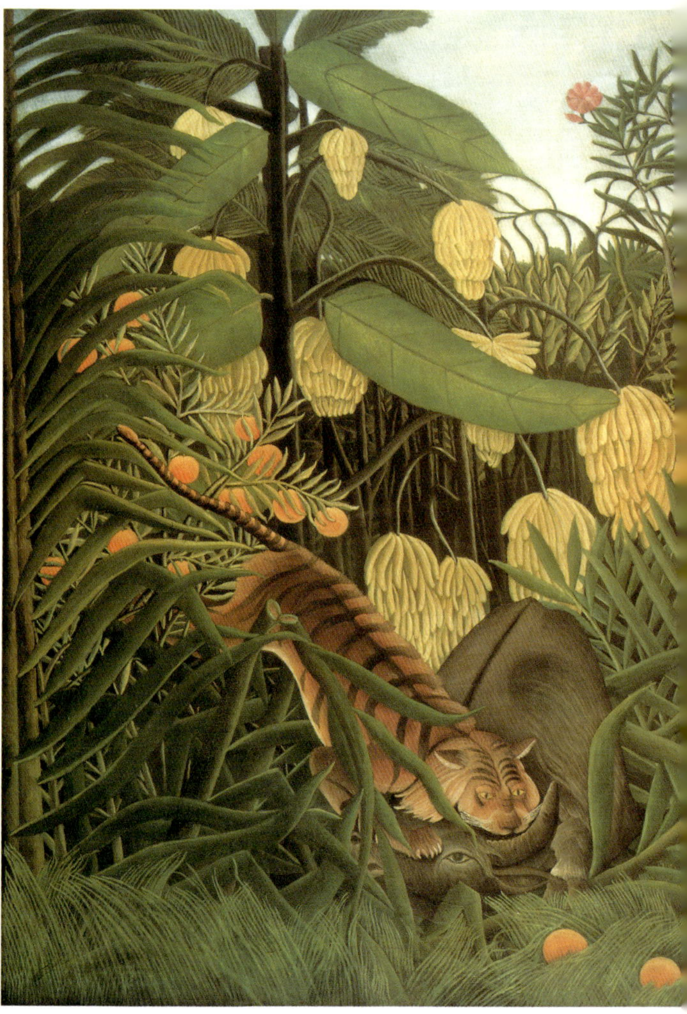

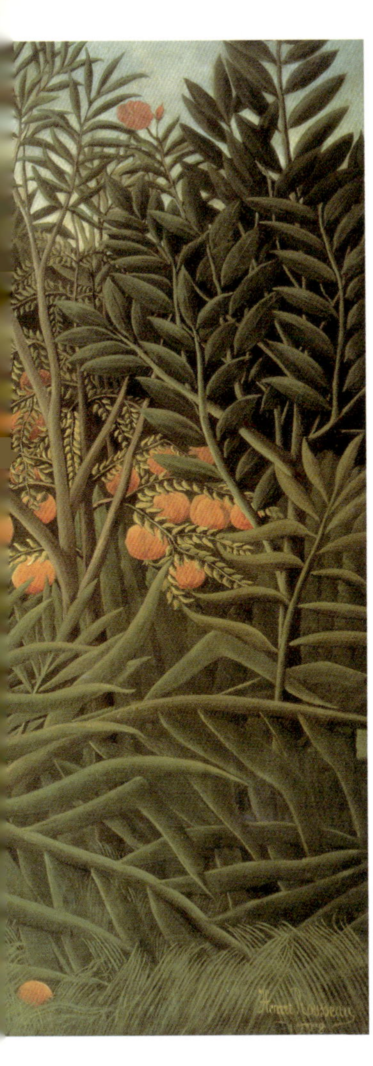

Fight Between a Tiger and a Buffalo 1908

Unpleasant Surprise 1901
Oil on canvas 193.2 x 129.5 CM

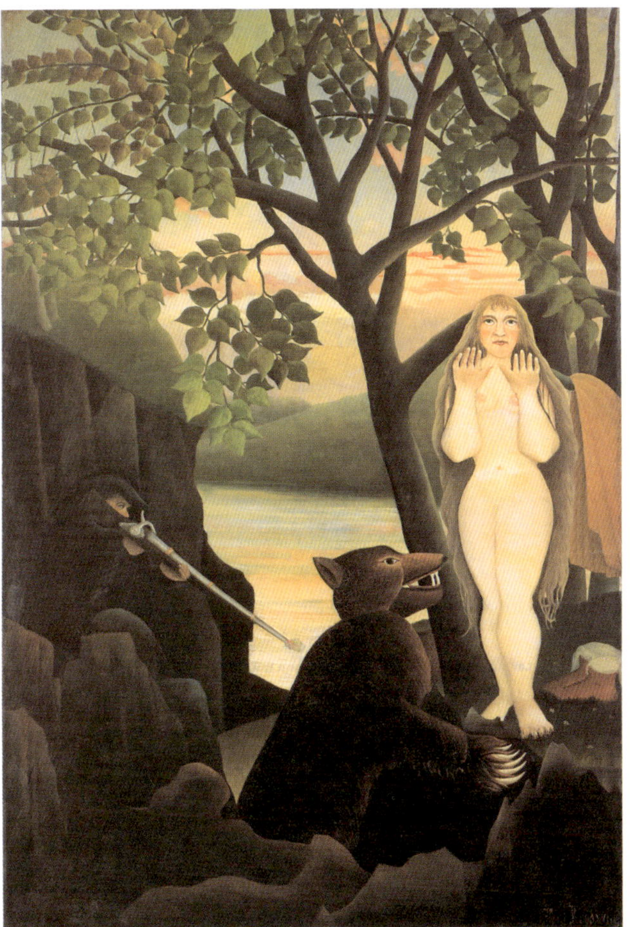

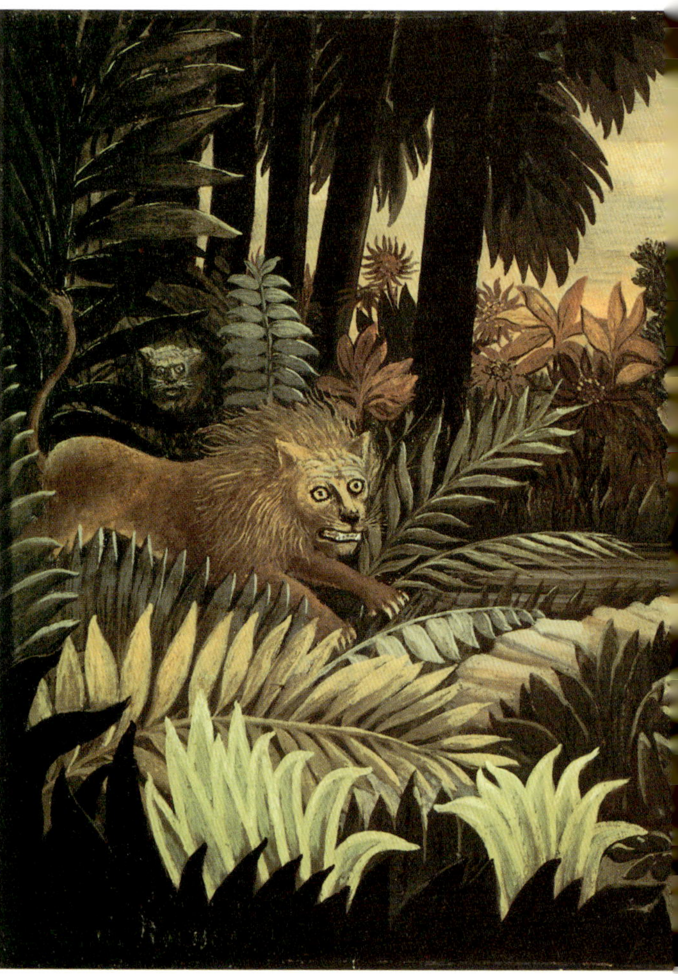

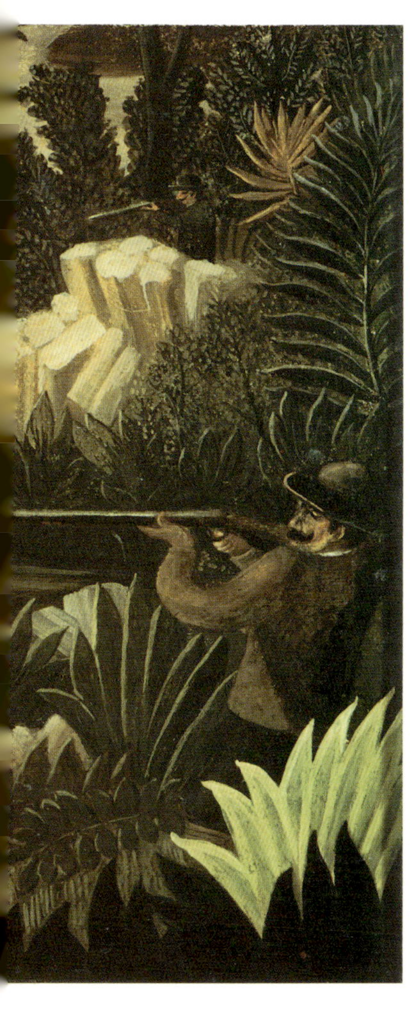

Lion Hunter c.1900
Oil on canvas 45 x 54 cm

Woman Walking in an Exotic Forest 1905
Oil on canvas 100 x 81 cm

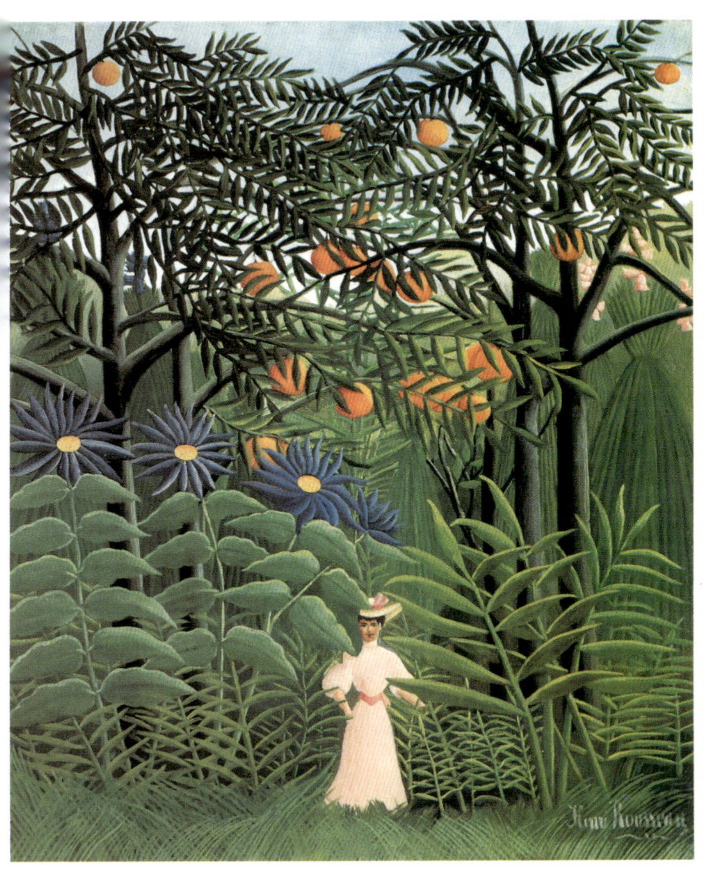

The Flamingos 1907
Oil on canvas 114 x 162 cm
(overleaf; detail opposite)

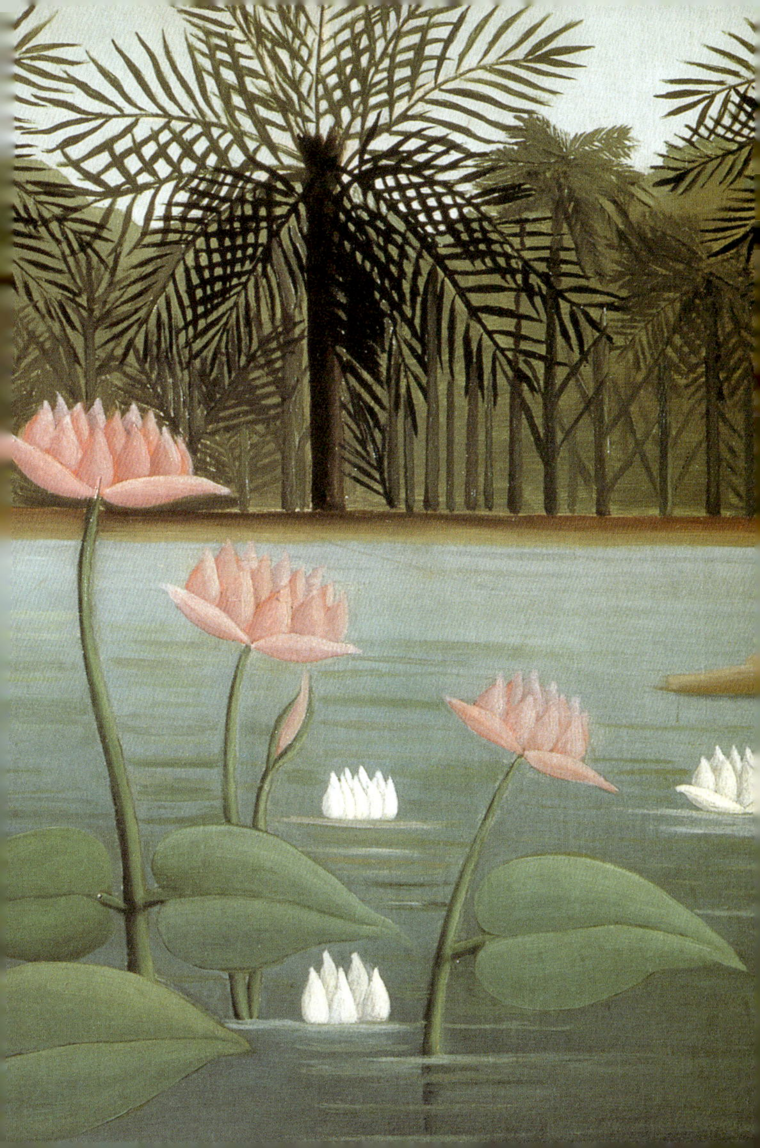

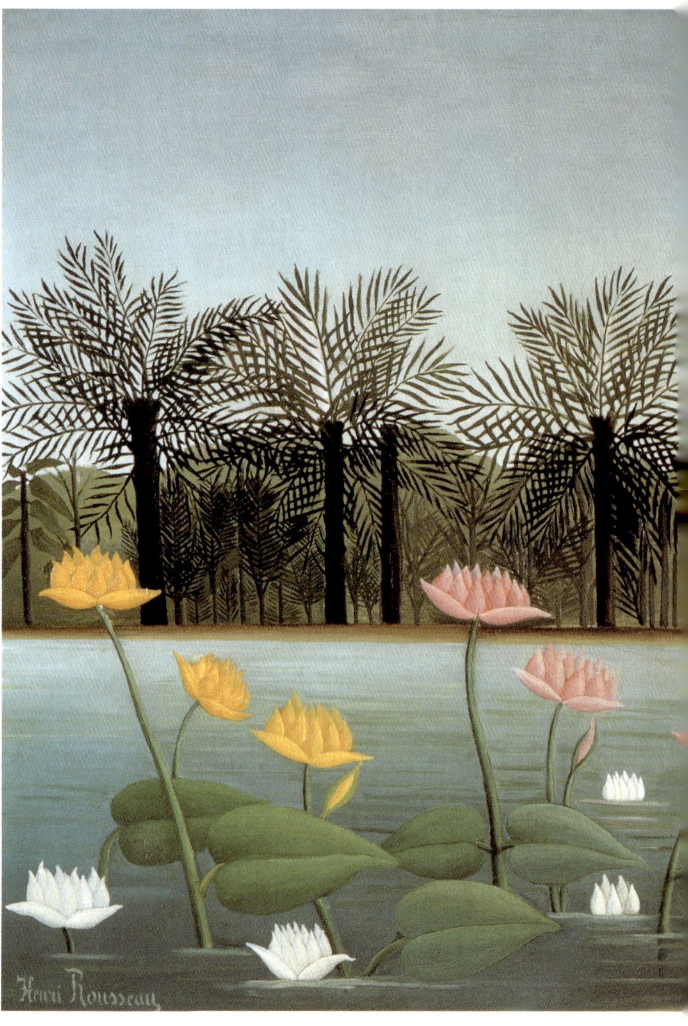
Henri Rousseau

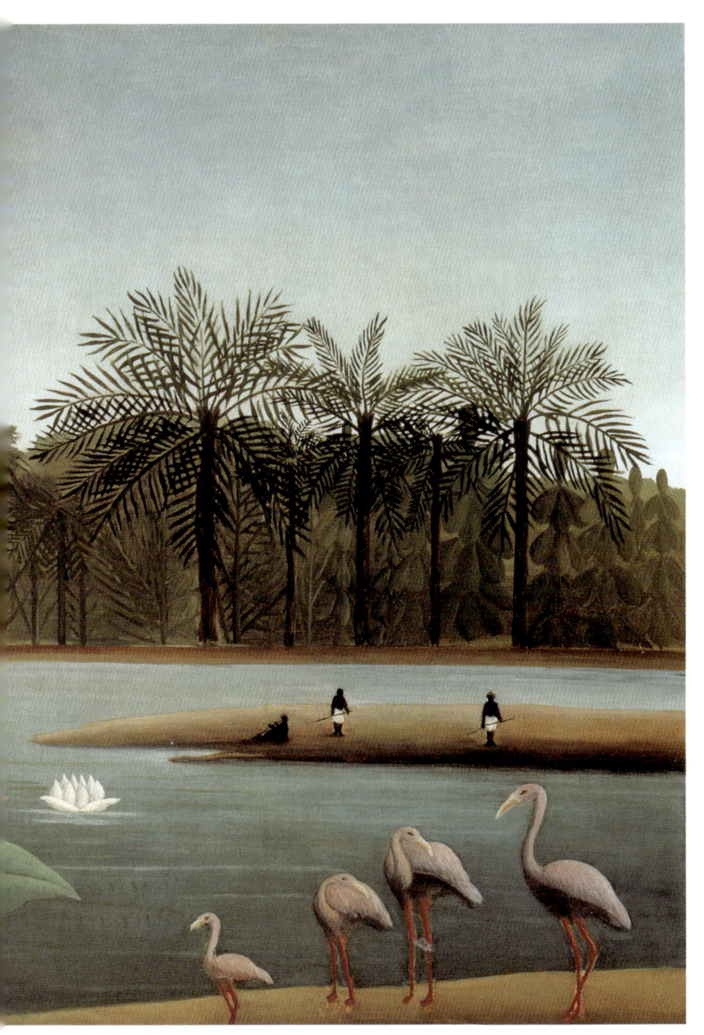

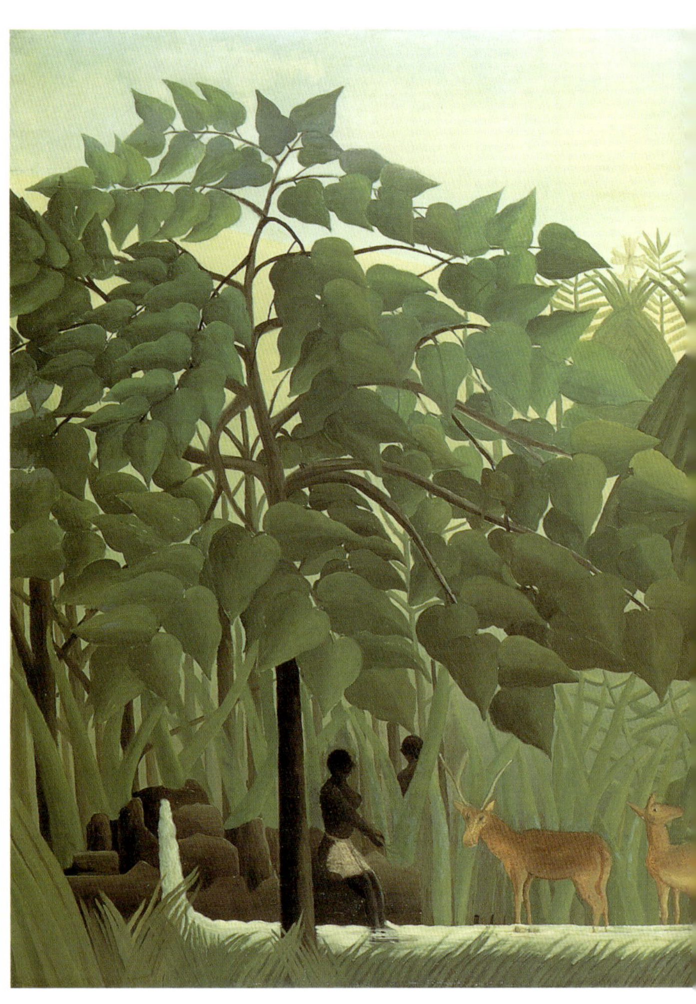

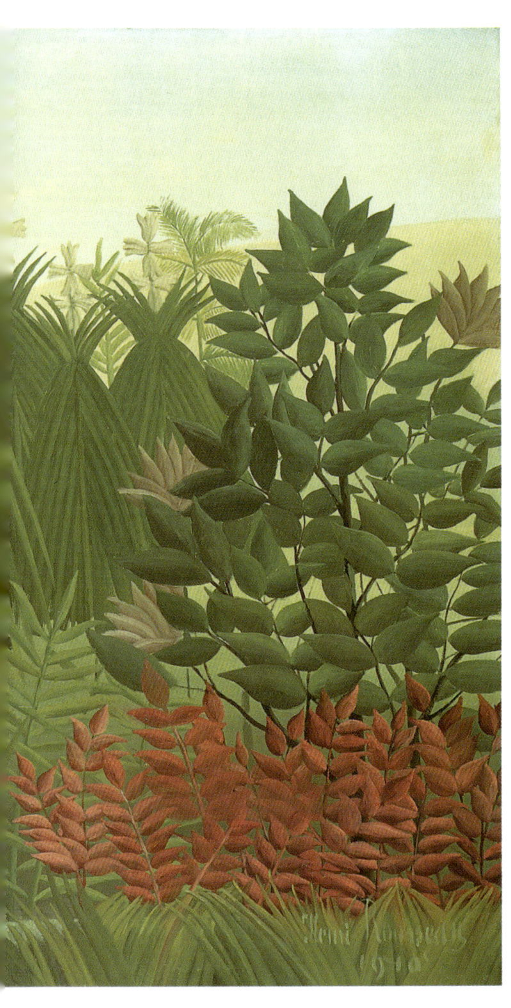

The Waterfall
1910
Oil on canvas
116 x 150 cm

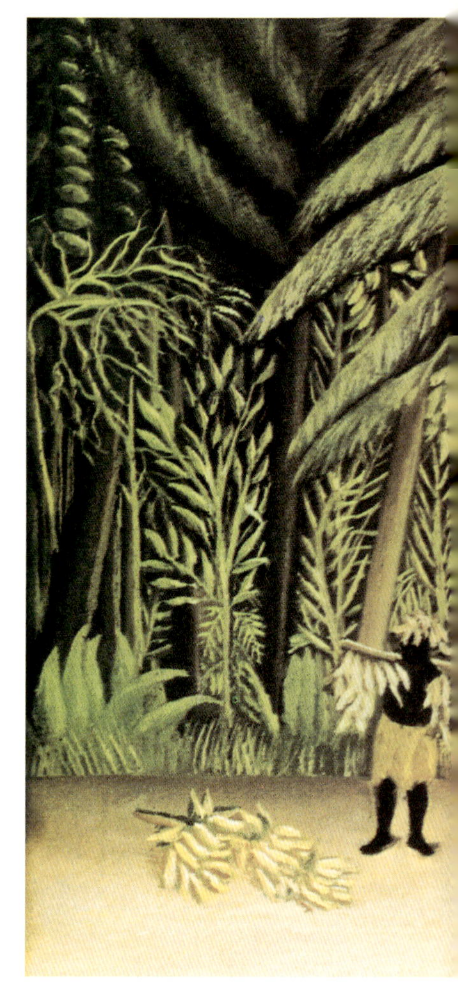

The Banana Plantation 1910
Oil on canvas
38 x 46 CM

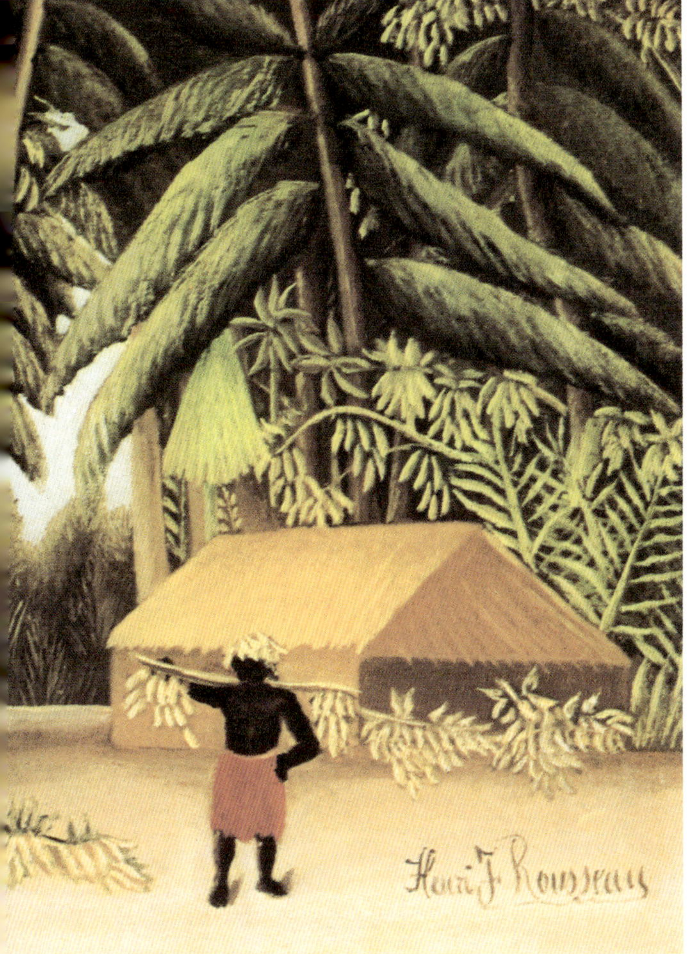
Henri J Rousseau

Zizi date unknown
Oil on canvas 21.5 x 14.5 cm

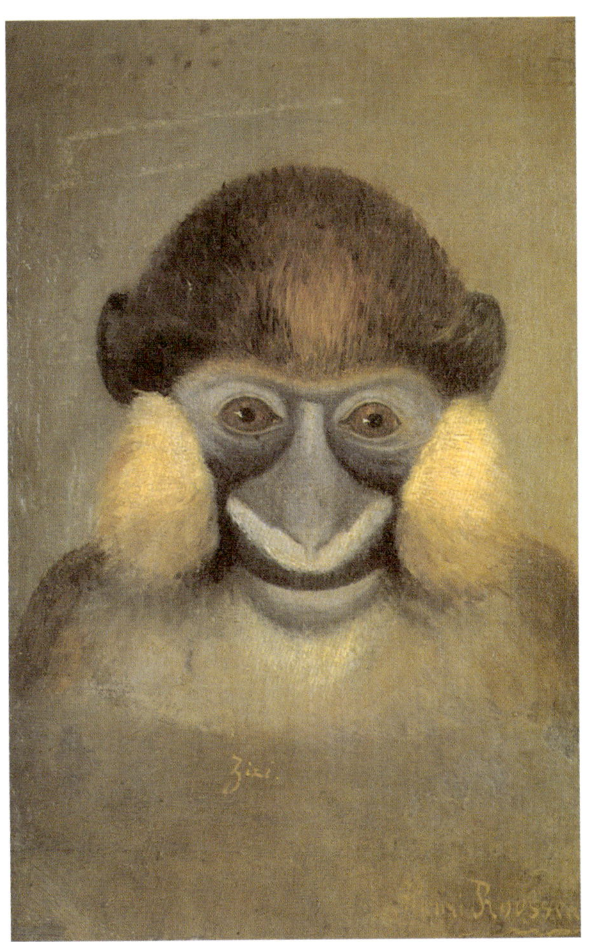
Zizi

The Merry Jesters 1906
Oil on canvas 146 x 114 CM

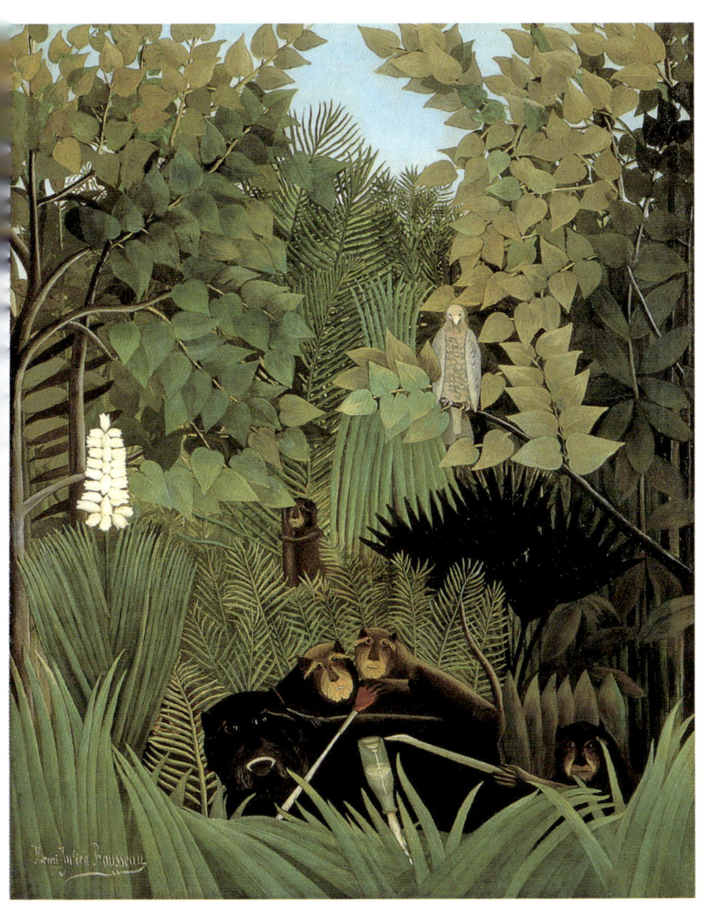
Henri Julien Rousseau

Tropical Forest with Monkeys 1910
Oil on canvas 129.5 x 162.6 CM (DETAIL)

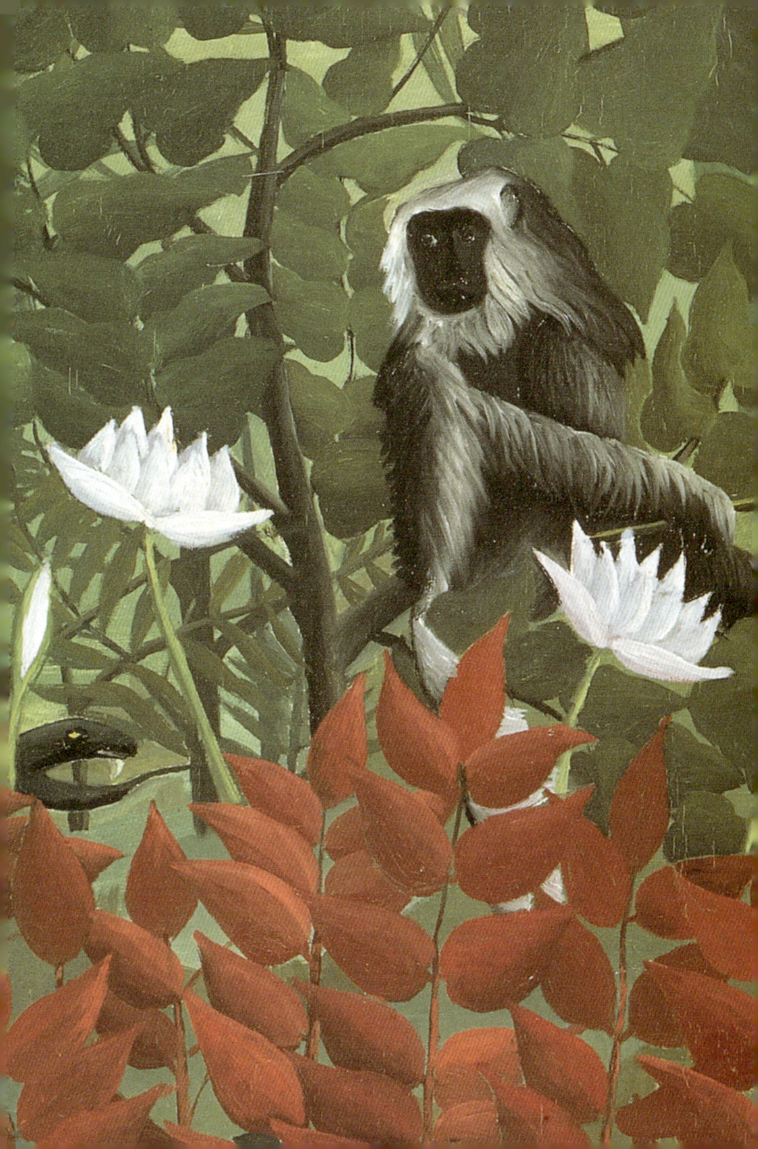

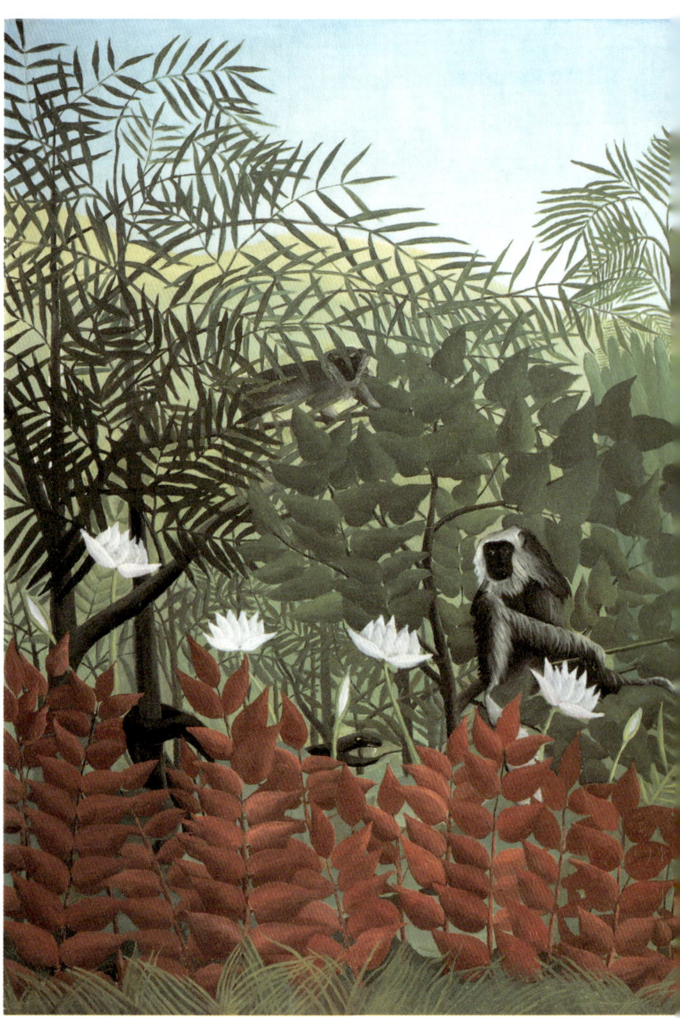

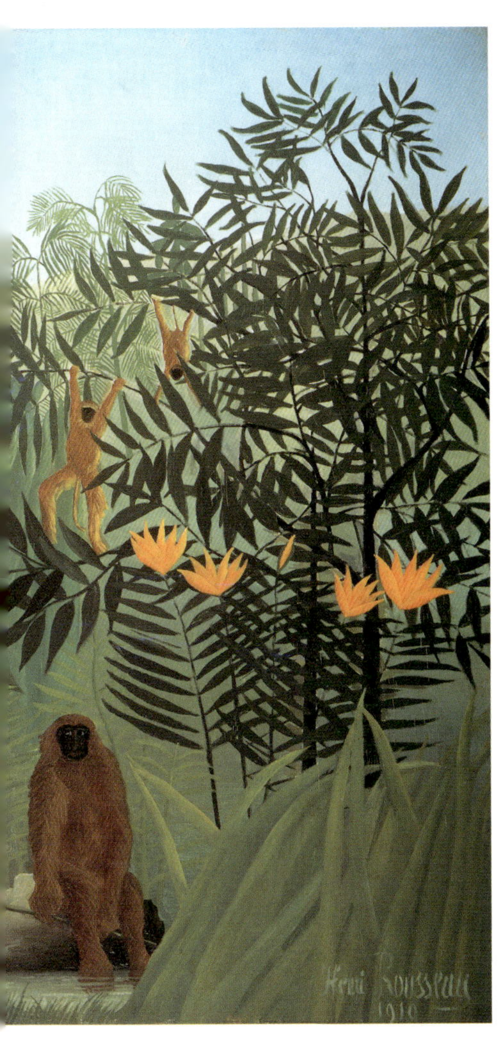

Tropical Forest with Monkeys
1910

Exotic Landscape 1908
Oil on canvas 116 x 89 CM

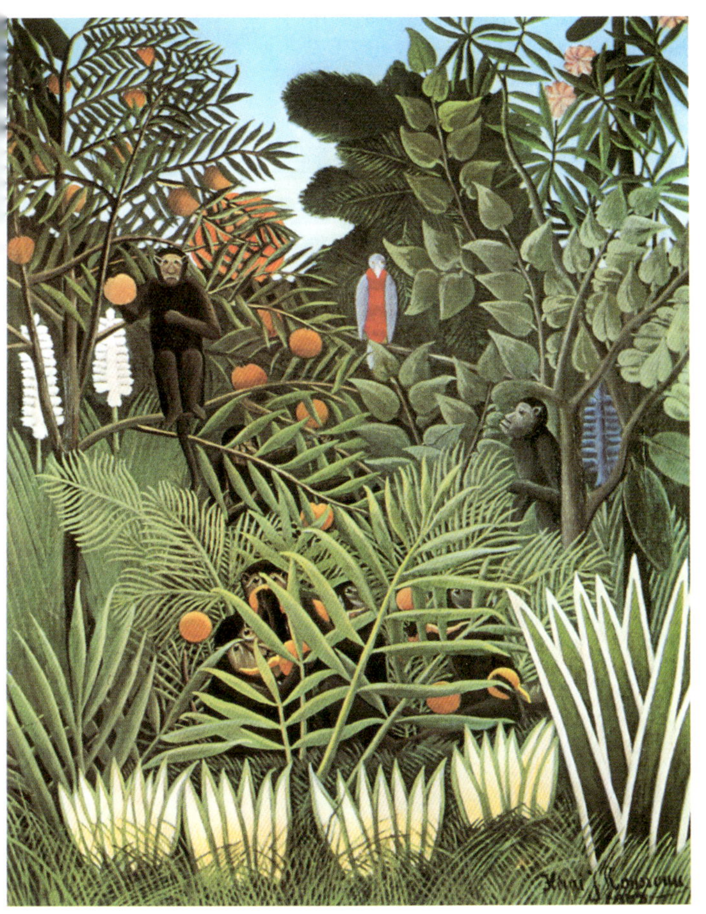

Exotic Landscape 1909
Oil on canvas 140.3 x 129.5 cm

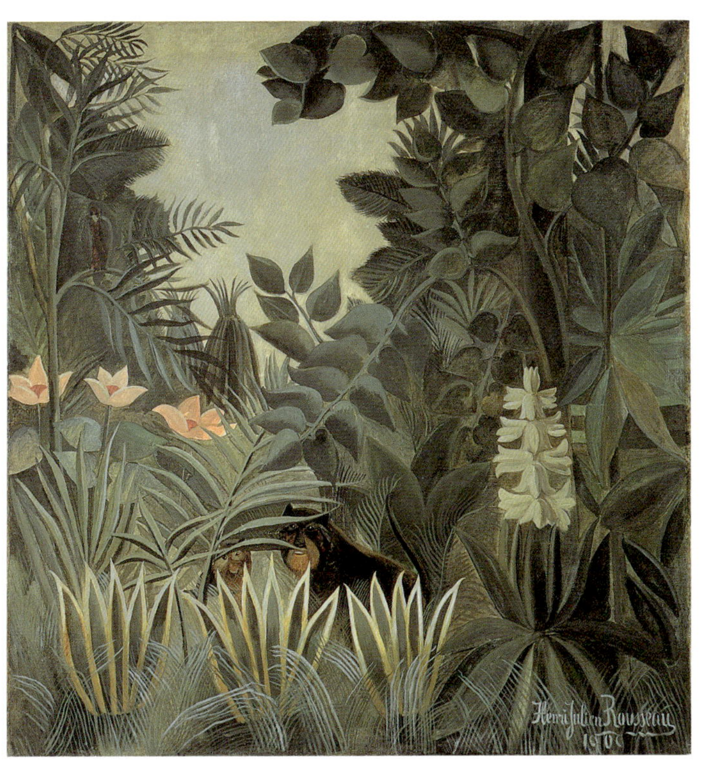
Henri Julien Rousseau

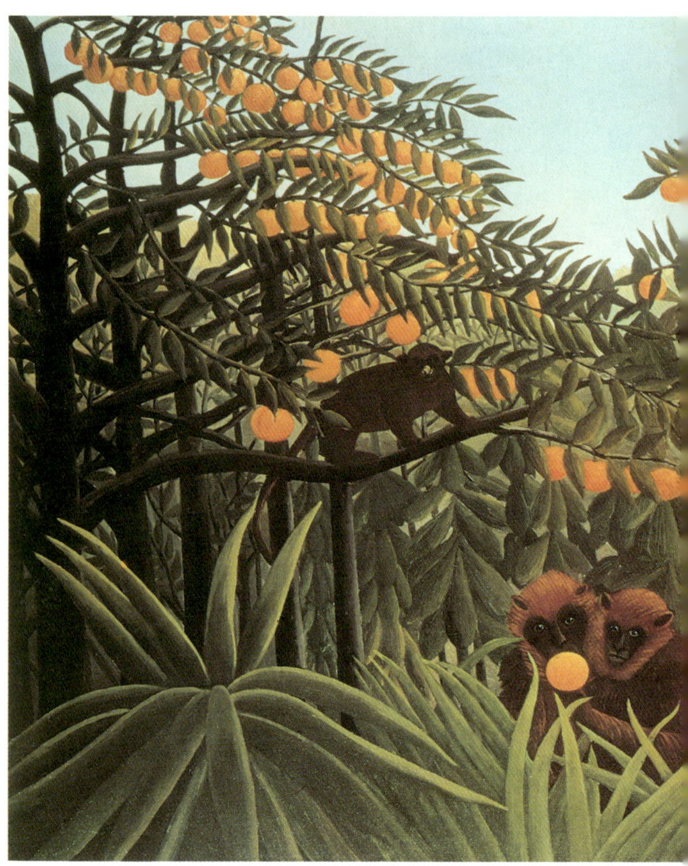

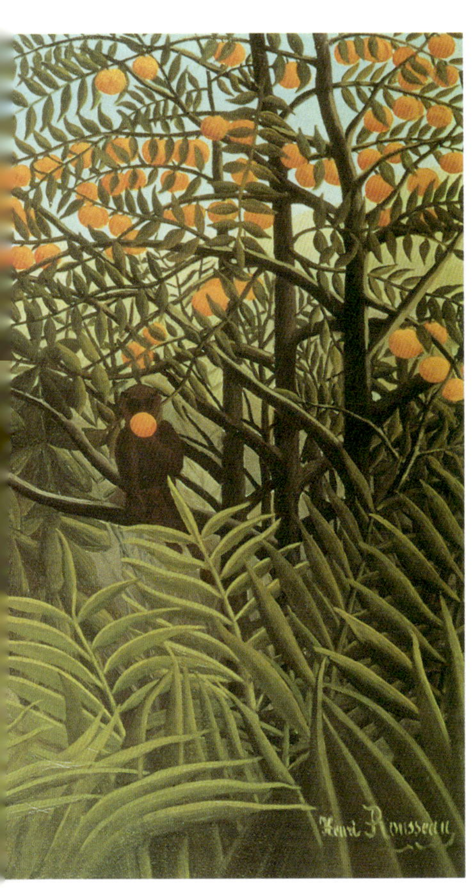

Monkeys in Orange Grove 1910
Oil on canvas 114 x 162 CM

Exotic Landscape 1910
Oil on canvas 130 x 162 CM
(DETAIL)

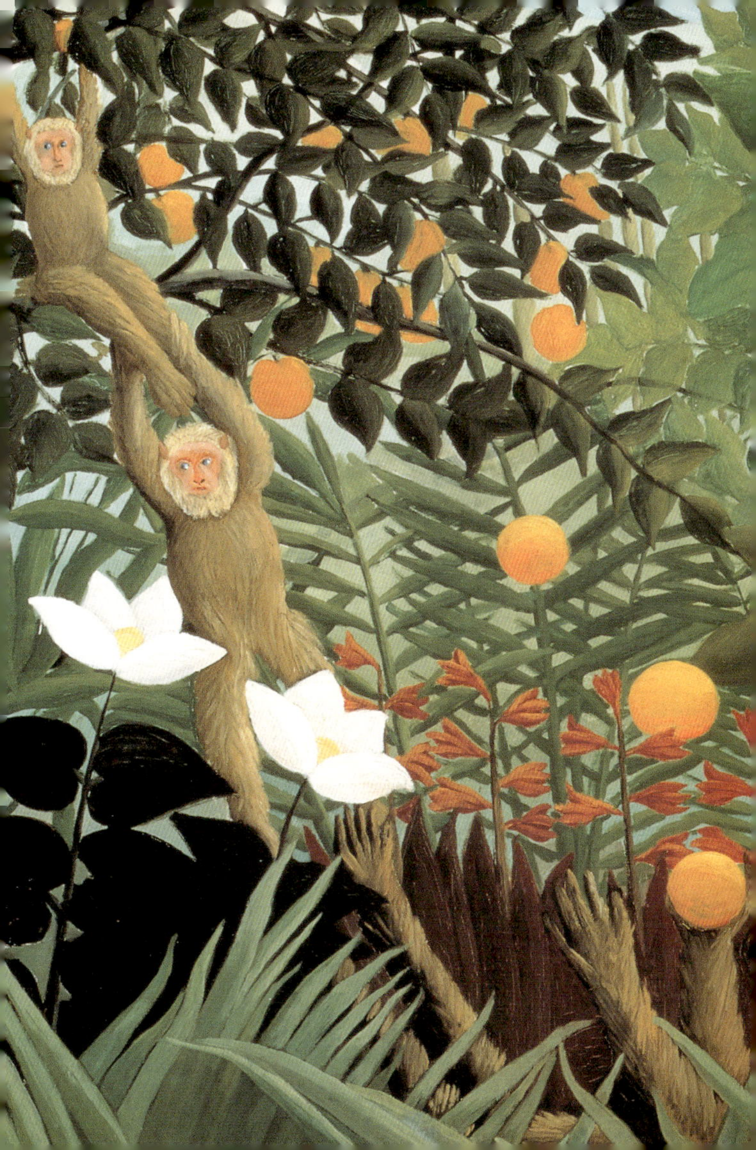

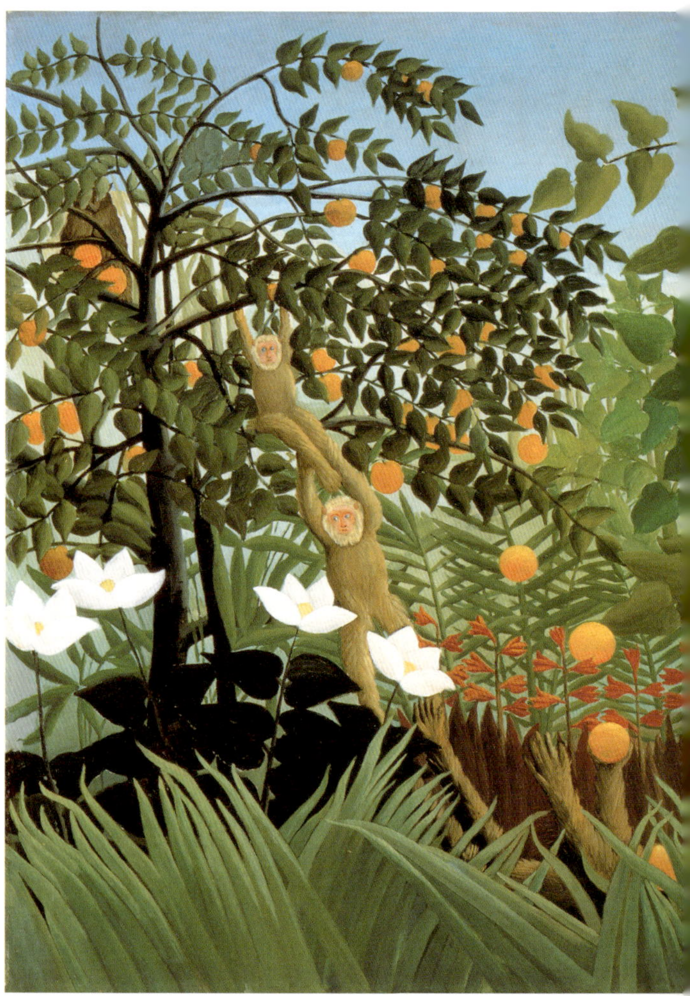

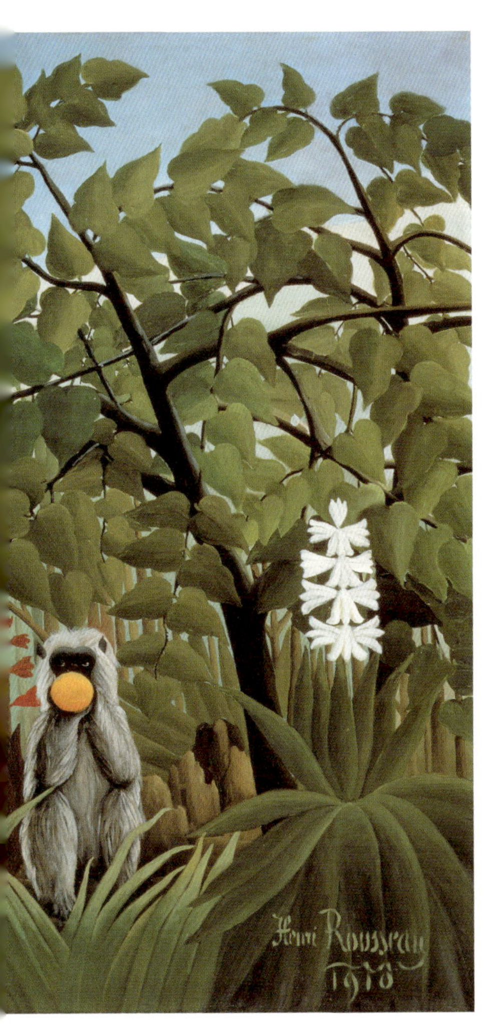

Exotic Landscape 1910

Tropical Landscape: An American Indian Struggling with a Gorilla 1910
Oil on canvas 114 x 162 cm (OVERLEAF; DETAIL OPPOSITE)

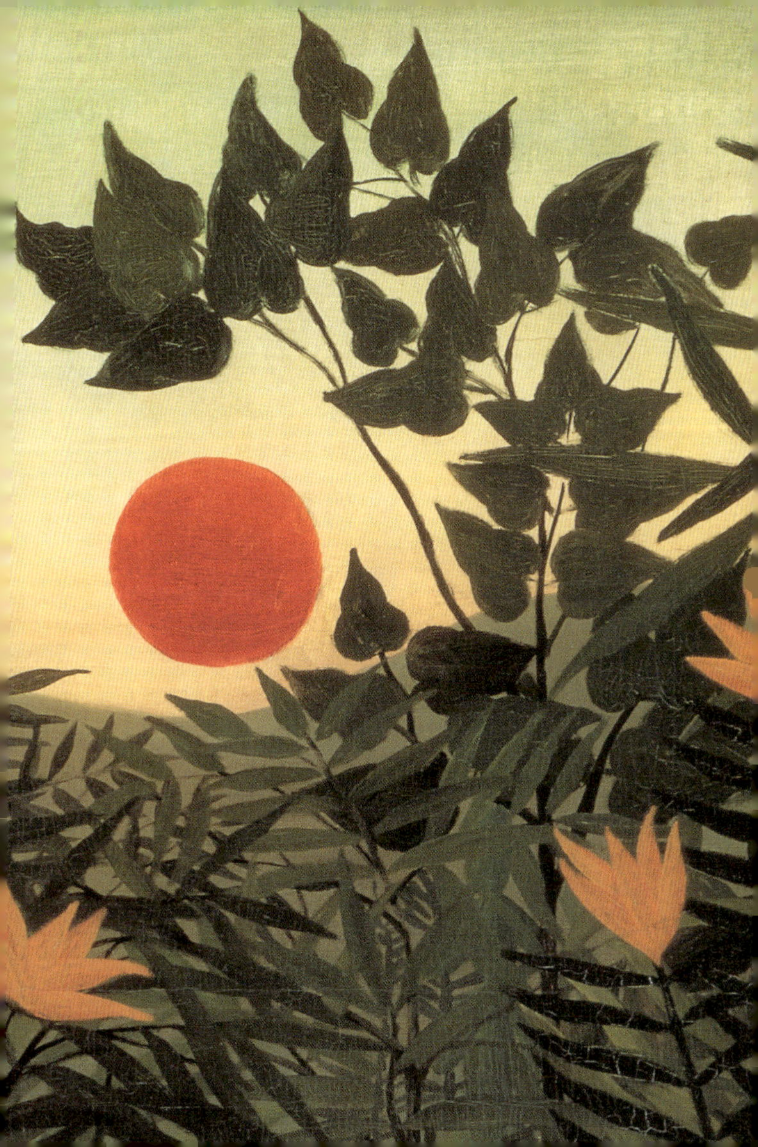

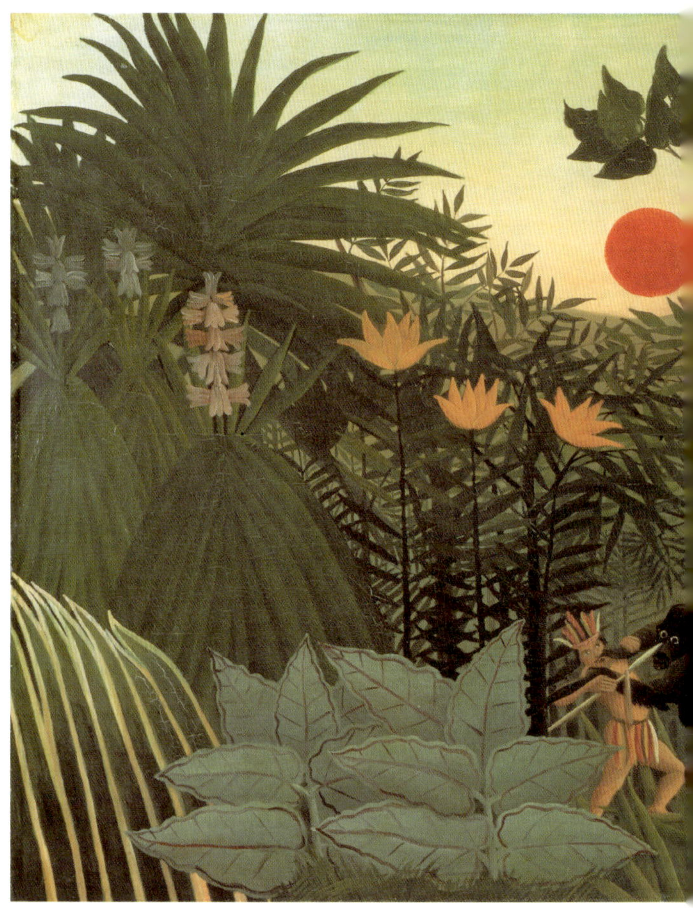

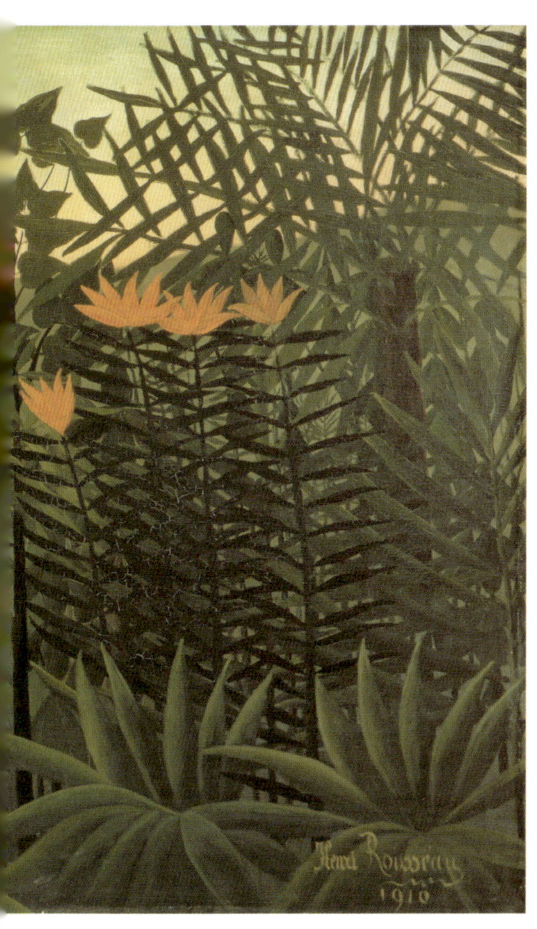

Horse Attacked by a Jaguar 1910
Oil on canvas 89 x 116 CM (DETAIL)

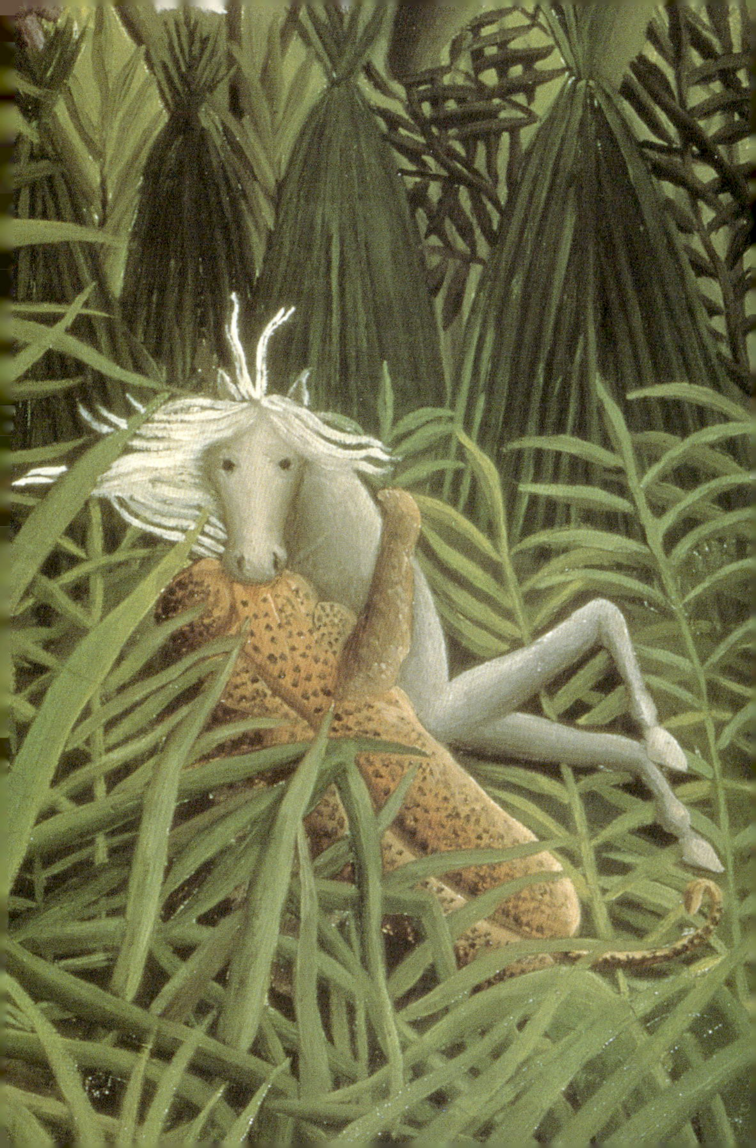

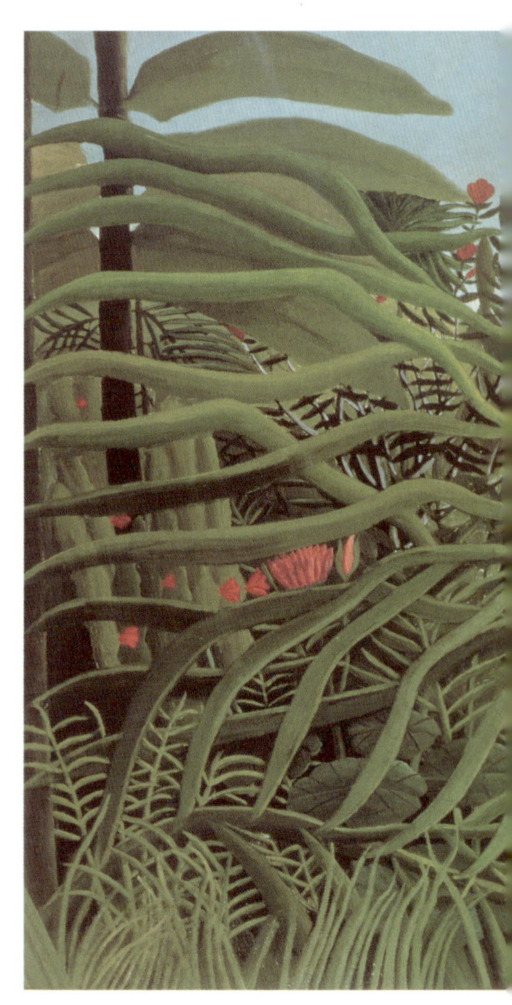

Horse Attacked by a Jaguar 1910

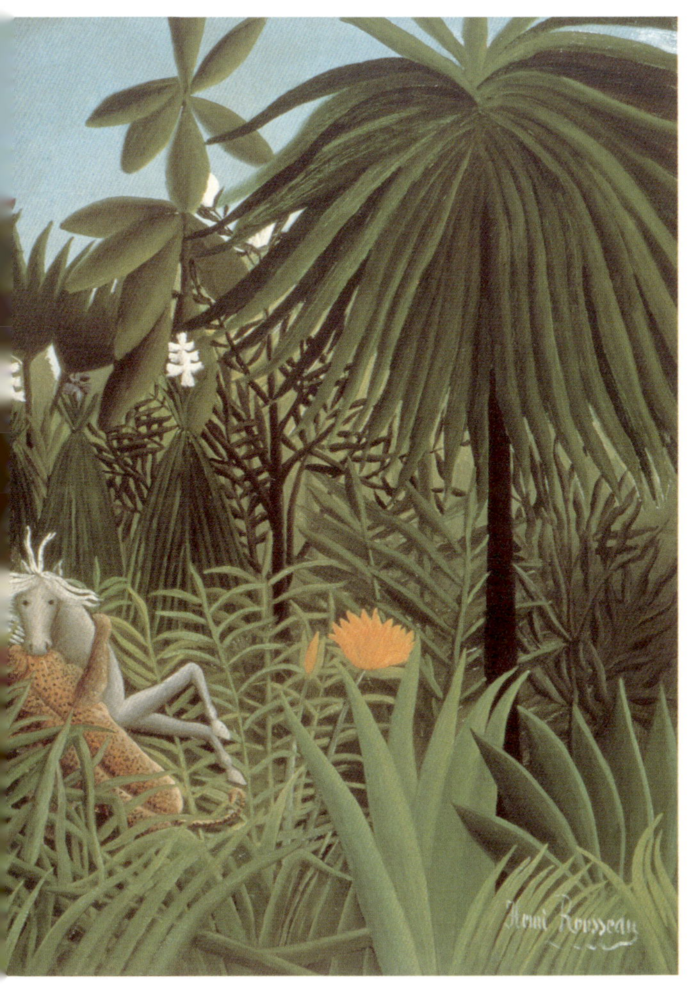
Henri Rousseau

Jungle Landscape with Setting Sun 1910
Oil on canvas 114 x 162.5 CM
(OVERLEAF; DETAIL OPPOSITE)

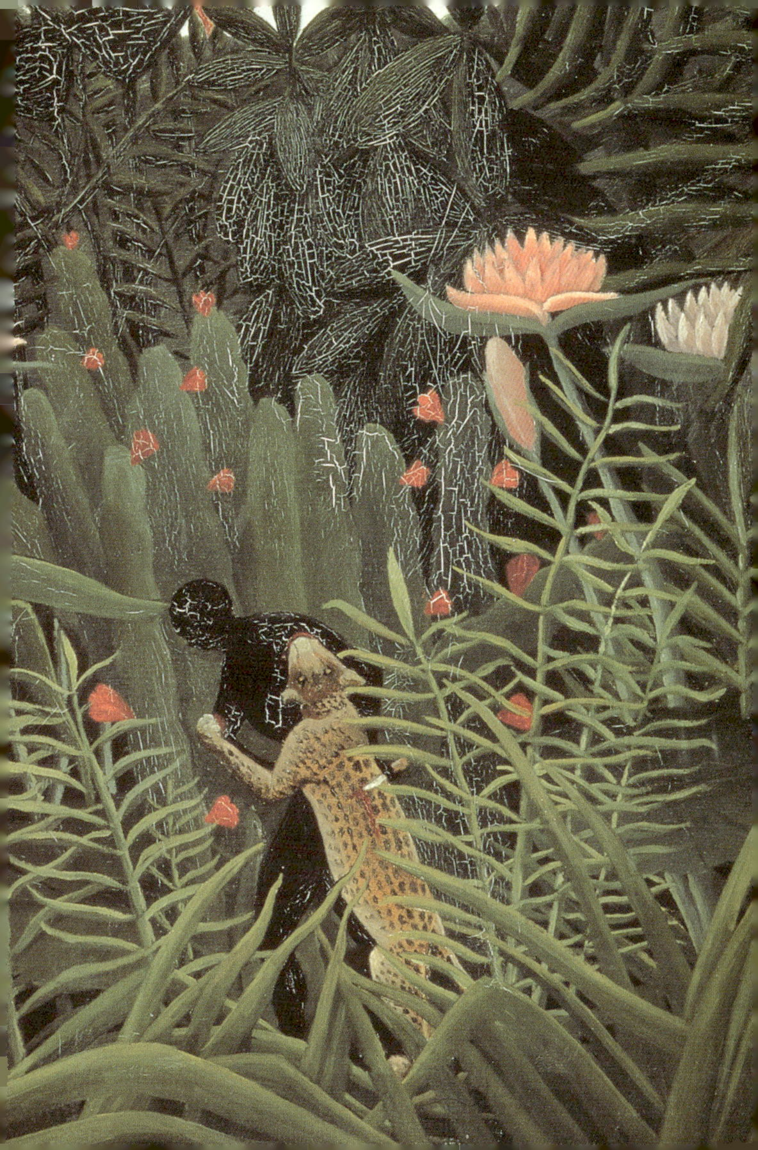

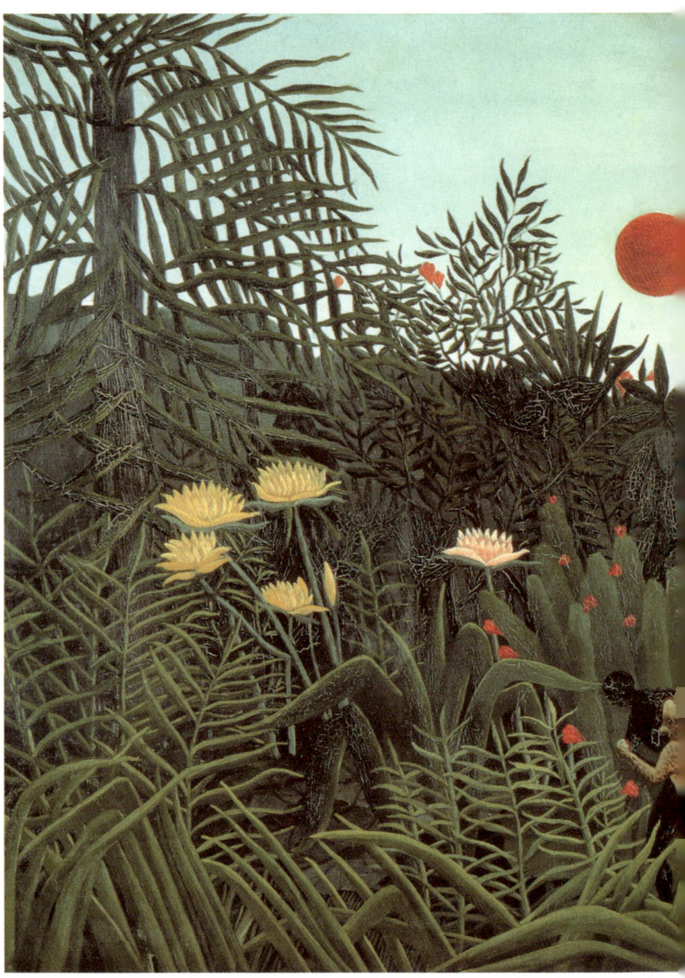

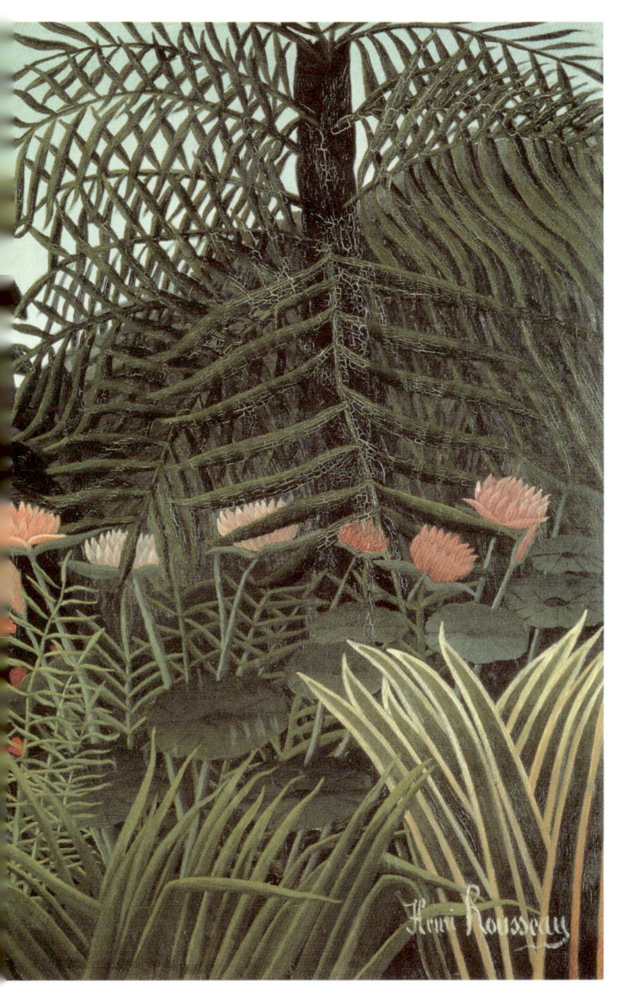
Henri Rousseau

Eve after 1904
Oil on canvas 61 x 46 CM

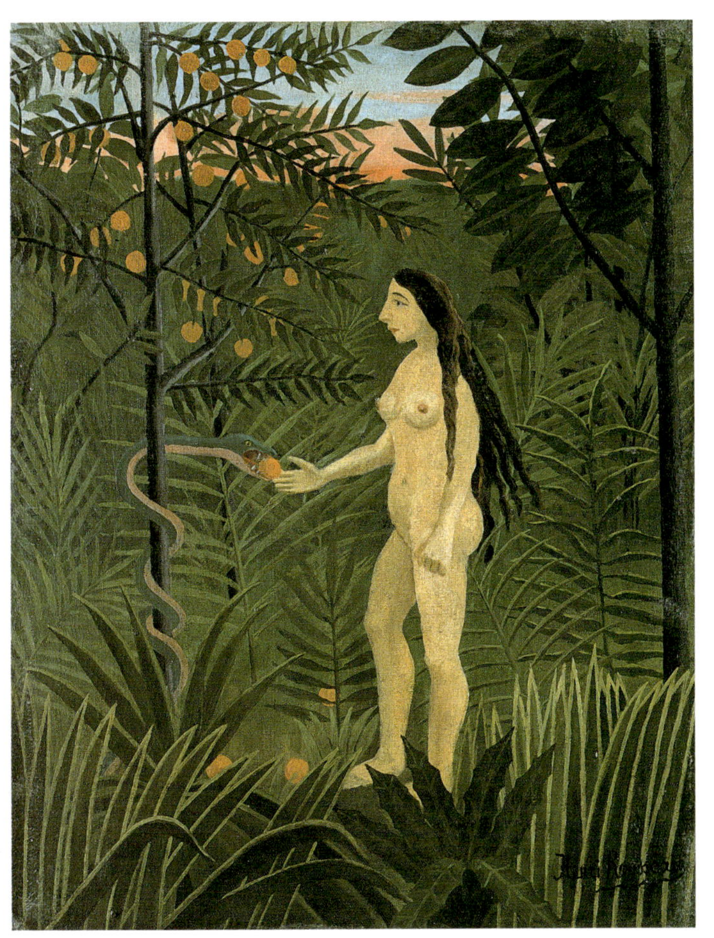

The Snake Charmer 1907
Oil on canvas 169 x 189.5 CM (DETAIL)

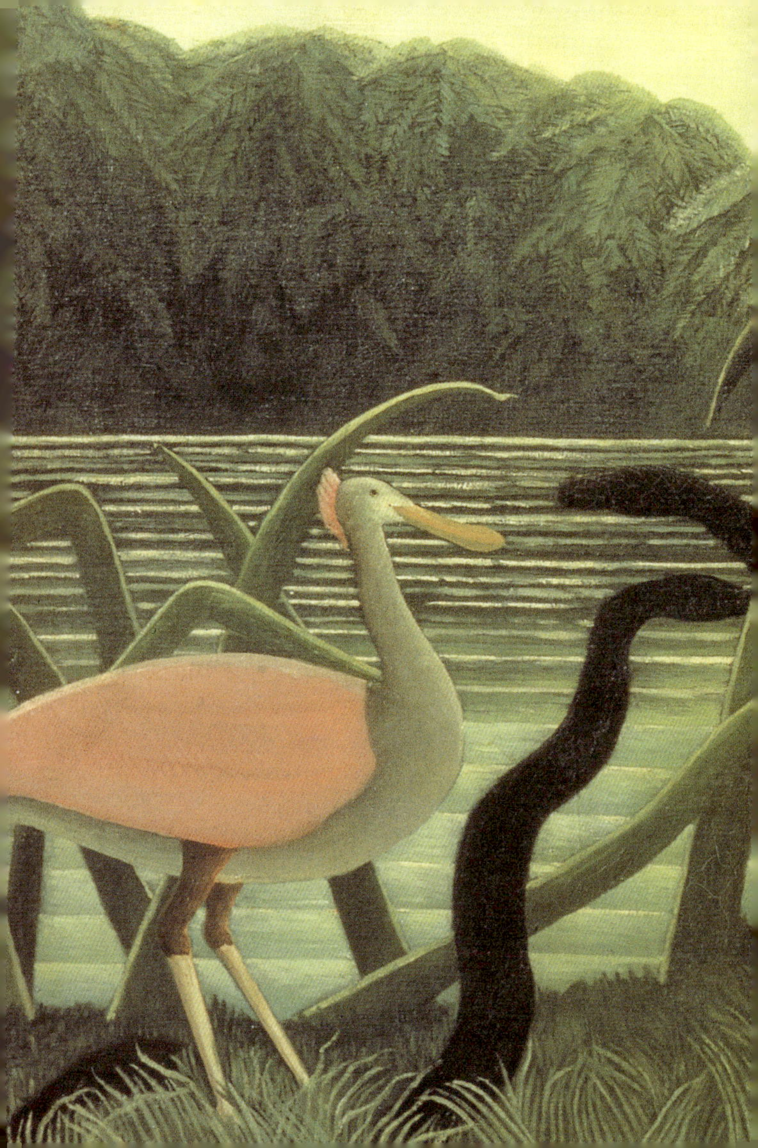

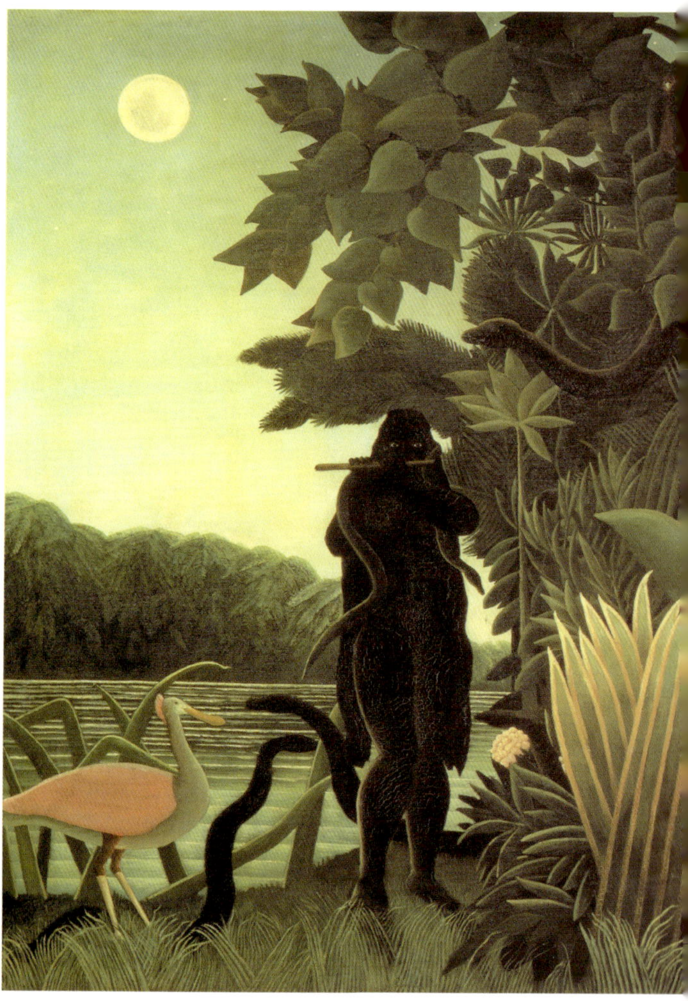

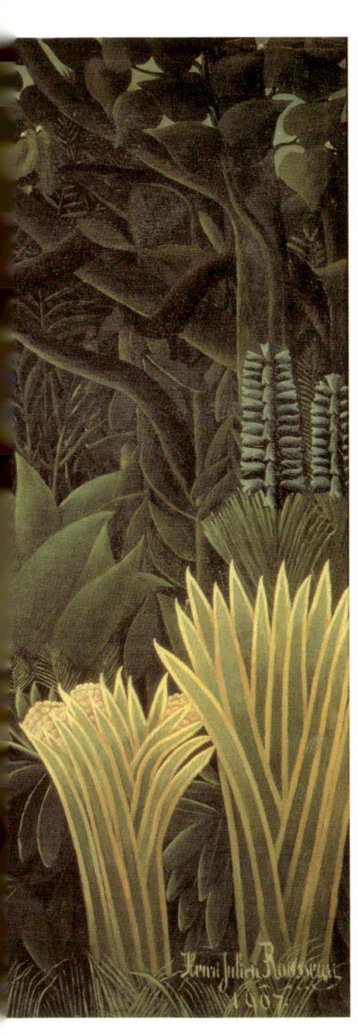

The Snake Charmer 1907

The Snake Charmer 1907 (DETAIL)

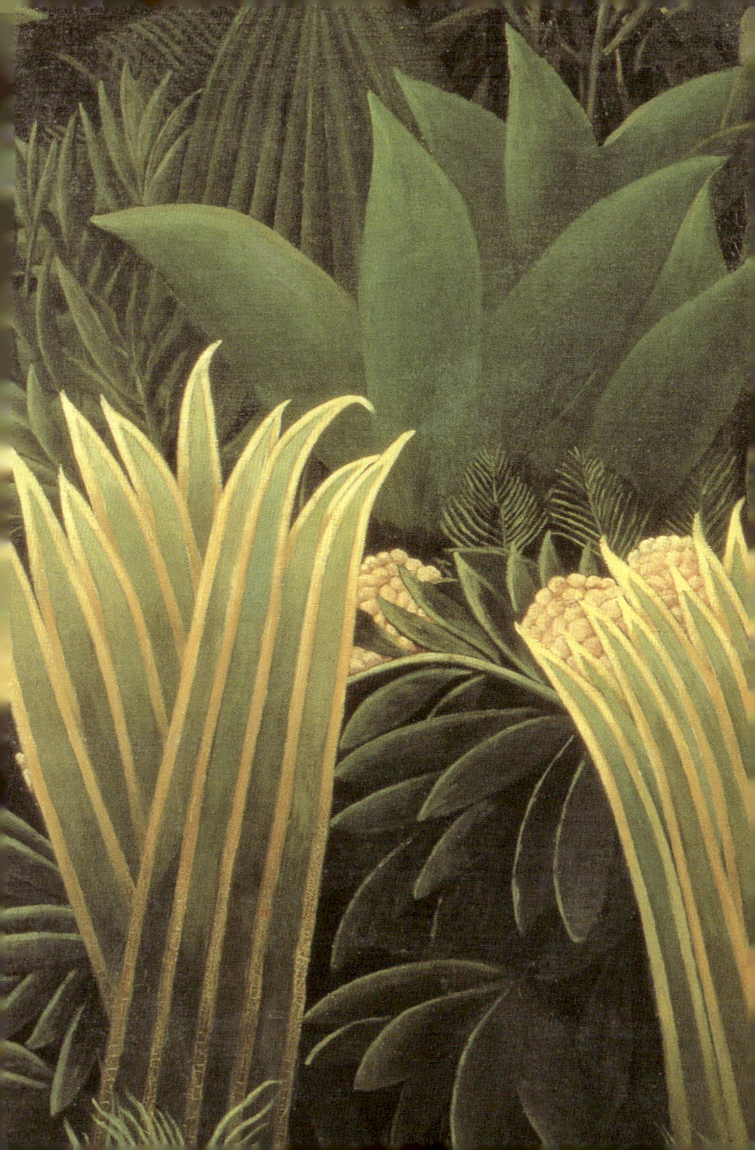

The Dream 1910
Oil on canvas 204.5 x 298 cm
(OVERLEAF; DETAIL OPPOSITE)

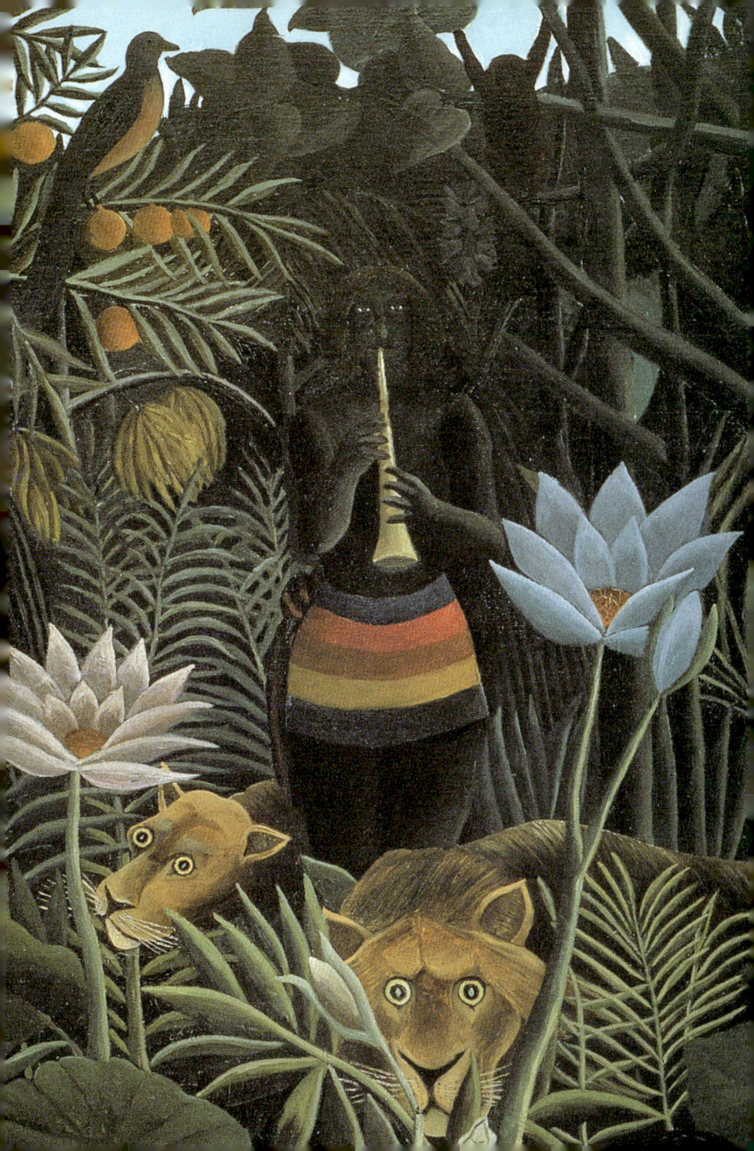

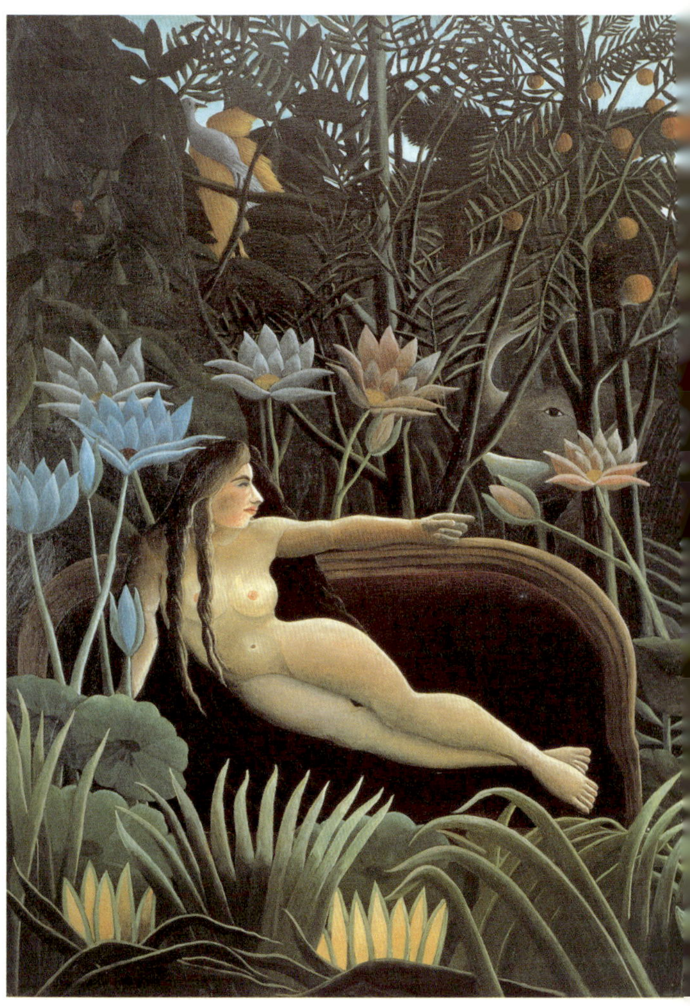

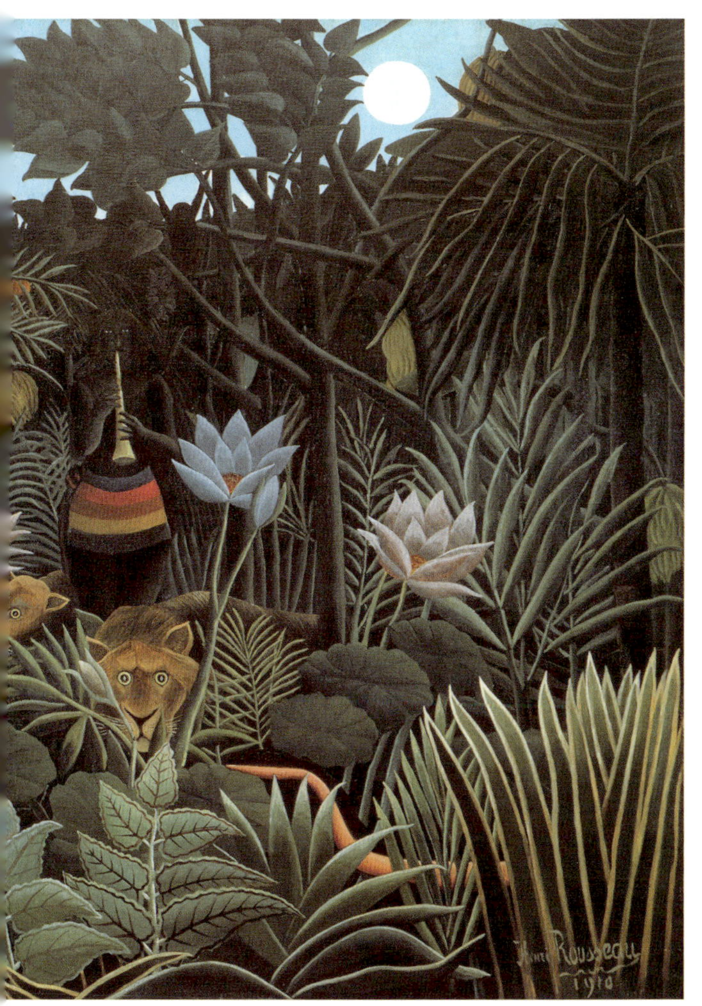
Rousseau
1910

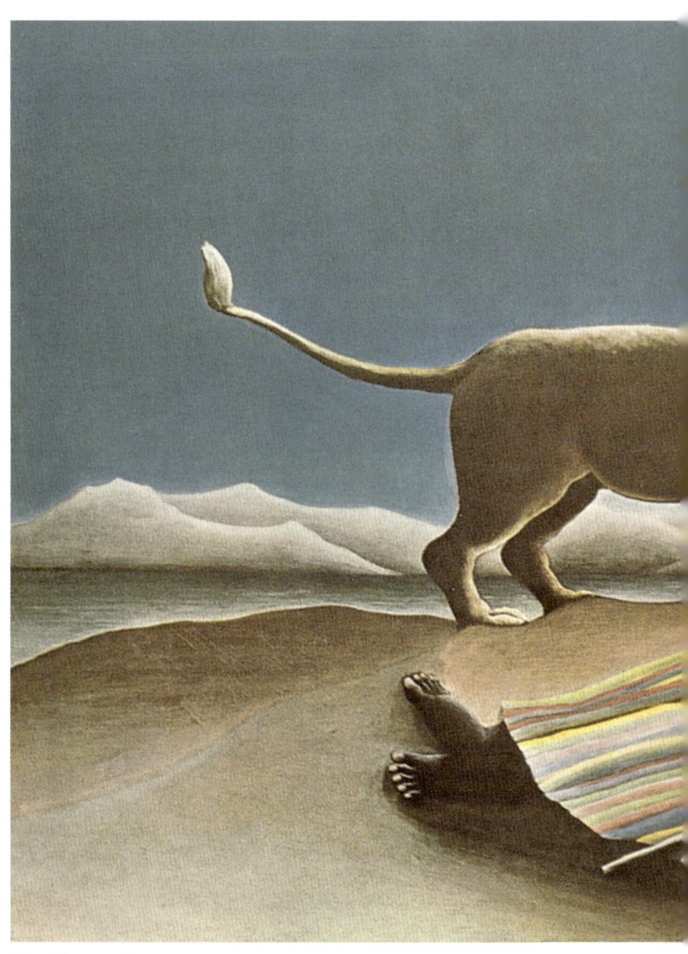

The Sleeping Gypsy 1897
Oil on canvas 129 x 200 cm

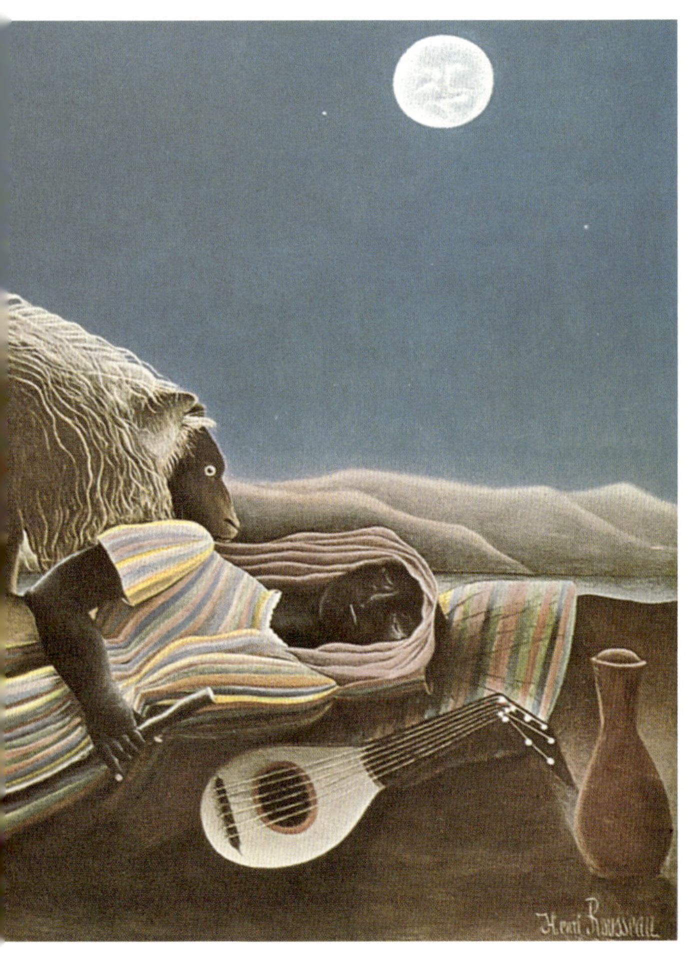
Henri Rousseau

Plates

Tiger in a Tropical Storm (Surprised!)
1891
Oil on canvas 130 x 162 cm
National Gallery, London

The Hungry Lion Throws Itself on the Antelope 1905
Oil on canvas 200 x 300 cm
Fondation Beyeler, Riehen/Basel, inv. no.88.4

Lion in the Jungle c.1904
Oil on canvas 38.4 x 46.5 cm
The Museum of Modern Art, New York, Lillie P. Bliss Collection

The Lion's Repast 1907
Oil on canvas 113.5 x 160 cm
Metropolitan Museum of Modern Art, New York, bequest of Samuel A. Lewisohn, 1951

Fight Between a Tiger and a Buffalo
1908
Oil on fabric 170 x 189.5 cm
Cleveland Museum of Art, Ohio, gift of the Hanna Fund, 1949.186

Unpleasant Surprise 1901
Oil on canvas 193.2 x 129.5 cm
The Barnes Foundation Collection, Merion, Pennsylvania, inv. no.281

Lion Hunter c.1900
Oil on canvas 45 x 54 cm
Private Collection
Photo: M. Coen

Woman Walking in an Exotic Forest
1905
Oil on canvas 100 x 81 cm
The Barnes Foundation Collection, Merion, Pennsylvania, inv. no.388

The Flamingos 1907
Oil on canvas 114 x 162 cm
Private Collection

The Waterfall 1910
Oil on canvas 116 x 150 cm
The Art Institute of Chicago, Helen Birch Bartlett Memorial Collection, 1962

The Banana Plantation 1910
Oil on canvas 38 x 46 cm
Paul Mellon Collection, Washington

Zizi date unknown
Oil on canvas 21.5 x 14.5 cm
G. Renand, Paris
Photo: G. Perron

The Merry Jesters 1906
Oil on canvas 146 x 114 cm
Philadelphia Museum of Art, Louise and Walter Arensberg Collection, 1950-134-176

Tropical Forest with Monkeys 1910
Oil on canvas 129 x 162.6 cm
National Gallery of Art, Washington, The John Hay Whitney Collection 1982, inv. no.1982.76.7

Exotic Landscape 1908
Oil on canvas 116 x 89 cm
Wertheimer Collection, New York

Exotic Landscape 1909
Oil on canvas 140.3 x 129.5 cm
National Gallery of Art, Washington

Monkeys in Orange Grove 1910
Oil on canvas 114 x 162 cm
Ms. Adelaide Milton de Groot, New York

Exotic Landscape 1910
Oil on canvas 130 x 162 cm
Norton Simon Foundation, Pasadena

Tropical Landscape: An American Indian Struggling with a Gorilla 1910
Oil on canvas 114 x 162 cm
Virginia Museum of Fine Arts, Mellon Collection

Horse Attacked by a Jaguar 1910
Oil on canvas 89 x 116 cm
Pushkin Museum of Fine Arts, Moscow

Jungle Landscape with Setting Sun 1910
Oil on canvas 114 x 162.5 cm
Öffentliche Kunstsammlung, Kunstmuseum Basel, inv. no.2225

Eve after 1904
Oil on canvas 61 x 46 cm
Hamburger Kunsthalle, property of the Stiftung zur Förderung der Hamburgischen Kunstsammlungen, inv. no.2992

The Snake Charmer 1907
Oil on canvas 169 x 189.5 cm
Musée d'Orsay, Paris

The Dream 1910
Oil on canvas 204.5 x 298 cm
The Museum of Modern Art, New York, gift of Nelson A. Rockefeller, 1954

The Sleeping Gypsy 1897
Oil on canvas 129 x 200 cm
The Museum of Modern Art, New York, gift of Mrs Simon Guggenheim, 1939

Biography

1844 Henri Julien Félix Rousseau is born 21 May in Laval, capital of the department of Mayenne in western France. He is the third of four children of Julien Rousseau, ironmonger, and his wife Eléonore.

1849–1860 Attends school in Laval. Leaves with distinction in music and drawing.

1861 The family moves to Angers.

1863 Is employed by the lawyer Fillon. Although exempt from military service, volunteers for seven years in the army when charged with embezzlement.

1864 Serves a one-month prison sentence in Nantes and in March continues his army service with the fifty-second Infantry Regiment, stationed in Caen.

1867 Return of the two battalions of his regiment that took part in the Mexico expedition. Later apocryphal tales to the effect that Rousseau went to Mexico with them must have originated in his comrades' stories, which he himself liked to tell.

1868 Death of his father. Rousseau leaves the army early and moves to Paris. Finds a position with the bailiff Radez.

1869 Marries the 18-year-old seamstress Clémence Boitard.

1870 Birth of their first son. Outbreak of the Franco-Prussian War. Mobilisation on 14 July, Napoleon III declares war on Prussia on 20 July. Rousseau is called up as a reservist but is back at home in mid-September without seeing any fighting.

1871 Death of Rousseau's son. He gets a job as a clerk at the Paris toll service – a minor civil service post – where he works imposing duty on goods coming in and out of the city.

1872 First self-taught attempts at painting may date from this year.

1876 Birth of Julia Rousseau, the only one of his seven children to live (died 1956).

1884 On the recommendation of the painter Félix Clément, Rousseau receives a permit to copy works of art in the Louvre, the Musée de Luxembourg, and the palaces of Versailles and Saint-Germain.

1885 Exhibits two of his pictures in public for the first time.

1886 Exhibits at the Salon des Indépendants – the jury-free salon for independent artists – showing four pictures.

1887 Exhibits three pictures at the third Salon des Indépendants. The critics receive them favourably, comparing him to painters of the early Italian Renaissance.

1888 Exhibits five pictures at the fourth Salon des Indépendants. Clémence Rousseau dies of tuberculosis at the age of thirty-seven.

1889 Is so impressed by the Paris World Exposition that he writes a 'vaudeville play' in three acts and ten scenes: *Une visite à l'Exposition de 1889*. Exhibits three pictures at the fifth Salon des Indépendants.

1890 Exhibits drawings and five pictures at the sixth Salon des Indépendants, including his self-portrait *Myself, Portrait-Landscape* 1890. His works are shown alongside Paul Gauguin's. Rousseau's mother dies in Angers.

1891 Exhibits seven paintings at the seventh Salon des Indépendants, including the first jungle picture, *Tiger in a Tropical Storm (Surprised!)*. They are praised by Félix Vallotton. The city of Paris awards him a silver medal by mistake, as the result of mixing up two names. Subsequently Rousseau describes himself as 'medallist' on his visiting cards.

1892 Exhibits six works at the eighth Salon des Indépendants. They are praised by Arsène Alexandre.

1893 Represented by five pictures at the ninth Salon des Indépendants. He applies to leave his post at the toll service, and retires in December.

1894 Exhibits four pictures at the tenth Salon des Indépendants, including one of his major works, *War* 1894. Becomes friends with the writer Alfred Jarry, who also comes from Laval.

1895 His lithograph after the painting *War* is published in the second edition of *L'Ymagier*, a journal edited by Jarry and Rémy de Gourmond. Exhibits ten works at the eleventh Salon des Indépendants. Writes an autobiographical article (which was not published) for the second volume of the series *Portraits du prochain siècle (Portraits of the Next Century)*. At around this time, he plays in an amateur orchestra and earns some money as a street musician.

1896 Exhibits ten pictures at the twelfth Salon des Indépendants.

1897 Exhibits nine pictures at the thirteenth Salon des Indépendants, including *The Sleeping Gypsy*. They are well received by Thadée Natanson in the journal *La Revue blanche.* Jarry lodges with Rousseau for a short time.

1898 Exhibits five pictures at the fourteenth Salon des Indépendants. He offers the mayor of Laval *The Sleeping Gypsy* for around 2,000 francs. The sale does not take place. Rousseau may well have made friends with the painter Mérodack-Jeanneau and have taken part in the spiritualist séances of the Rosicrucians. Moves to a studio apartment in the rue Vercingétorix.

1899 Writes a drama in five acts and nineteen scenes: *La Vengeance d'une orpheline russe (The Vengeance of a Russian Orphan Girl)*. Marries Joséphine-Rosalie Noury, a widow.

1900 Visits the Paris World Exposition and the retrospective exhibition *A Century of French Art*.

1901 Moves to no.36 rue Gassendi, where his wife opens a stationery shop. She also offers Rousseau's works for sale. He is deeply in debt to the colourman Paul Foinet. Exhibits seven pictures at the seventeenth Salon des Indépendants. Auguste Renoir expresses his admiration.

1902 Rousseau exhibits nine pictures and one drawing at the eighteenth Salon des Indépendants. He becomes a teacher of porcelain and watercolour painting at the Association Philotechnique, an institution founded in 1848 to promote adult education.

1903 Joséphine, Rousseau's second wife, dies. He exhibits eight pictures at the nineteenth Salon des Indépendants. He also teaches miniature painting at the Association Philotechnique.

1904 Exhibits four pictures at the twentieth Salon des Indépendants, including the jungle picture *Scouts Attacked by a Tiger* 1904.

1905 Exhibits four pictures at the twenty-first Salon des Indépendants. For the first time he exhibits three pictures at the Salon d'Automne, founded in 1903, at the Grand Palais. Wide and positive reception of the jungle picture *The Hungry Lion Throws Itself on the Antelope.*

1906 Is represented by five pictures at the twenty-second Salon des Indépendants. Georges Courteline acquires two works for his Musée des Horreurs. Jarry introduces him to the poet and critic Guillaume Apollinaire. The art dealer Ambroise Vollard buys *The Hungry Lion* for 200 francs. Rousseau is represented at the fourth Salon d'Automne by the jungle picture *The Merry Jesters.*

1907 Exhibits six pictures at the twenty-third Salon des Indépendants. Meets the painter Robert Delaunay and the art dealer Wilhelm Uhde, his first biographer. Teaches music and drawing in his studio apartment to children from the neighbourhood, and holds soirées attended by the young artists of the avant-garde who admire him: Delaunay, Apollinaire, Picasso, Braque, Brancusi, and others. Exhibits four pictures at the fifth Salon d'Automne, including *The Snake Charmer*, commissioned by Delaunay's mother, and two more exotic landscapes. Meets the American painter Max Weber. Is arrested on 2 December for a bank fraud in which he has become involved. Is freed provisionally on 31 December.

1908 Exhibits four pictures at the twenty-fourth Salon des Indépendants, including *Fight Between a Tiger and a Buffalo*. Does not exhibit at the Salon d'Automne. Picasso buys Rousseau's *Portrait of a Woman* c.1985 from a junk dealer in Montmartre. Picasso holds the legendary 'Rousseau Banquet' at his studio in the Bateau Lavoir; the guests include Georges Braque, Marie Laurencin, André Salmon, Max Jacob, Léo and Gertrude Stein. Rousseau gives a farewell party for Max Weber; those present include Picasso, Apollinaire, Fernande Olivier and the art dealer Joseph Brummer.

1909 Is given a suspended prison sentence of two years and fined 200 francs. Exhibits two pictures at the twentieth Salon des Indépendants. Vollard buys three pictures from him for 190 francs, including *Fight Between a Tiger and a Buffalo*. *The Merry Jesters* is shown at the Salon Izdelsky in Kiev and Odessa.

1910 Exhibits *The Dream* at the twentieth Salon des Indépendants; it creates a sensation. Commissions from Vollard, Hélène d'Oettingen, the Delaunays and Uhde follow. Vollard acquires *Horse Attacked by a Jaguar* for 100 francs. Several pictures are shown at the Salon Izdelsky in St Petersburg and Riga. On 2 September Rousseau dies of blood poisoning in the Necker hospital in Paris. The seven mourners at his funeral in Bagneux include Paul Signac and Robert Delaunay. Max Weber organises a small exhibition of works by Rousseau in his own possession at the 291 Gallery.

1911 A retrospective organized by Delaunay, with forty-seven of Rousseau's pictures, is held at the Salon des Indépendants. Uhde publishes the first monograph on him. Rousseau's picture *The Poultry Yard* 1896–8, owned by Kandinsky, is shown at the first exhibition held by the Blauer Reiter group in Munich.

1912 Through the sale of two portraits, and with the help of Le Dounaier's friends and admirers, Delaunay finances a thirty-year licence for Rousseau's grave. Apollinaire writes an inscription, which Brancusi transfers to the tombstone three years later.